LANDMARKS IN LITERATURE

Maynard Mack, *Series Editor*
Yale University

Some books belong to all times and places. They are the rivers, mountains, seas, and continents of our intellectual and moral world. They tell us where we are and how far we have still to go. They are, in short, our landmarks.

Landmarks in Literature is a series of interpretive studies of such books, each written by an authority of today, each a reference point between our present and our past.

EUGENE VANCE, author of this volume in the Landmarks in Literature series, received his Ph.D. from Cornell University, and did further studies of French medieval culture at the Universities of Poitiers and Strasbourg. He was a member of the English and French Departments at Yale University and is presently chairman of the Comparative Literature program at l'Université de Montréal and a director of research at the Institute of Medieval Studies at that university.

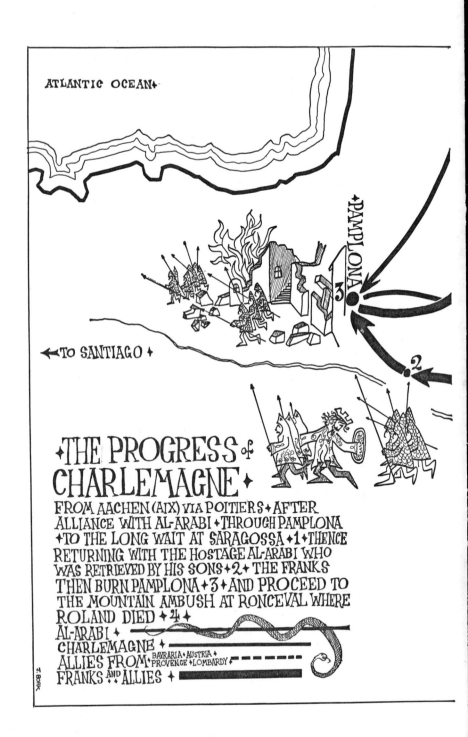

ATLANTIC OCEAN◄

PAMPLONA

◄TO SANTIAGO ◄

◄THE PROGRESS of CHARLEMAGNE◄

FROM AACHEN (AIX) VIA POITIERS ◄ AFTER
ALLIANCE WITH AL-ARABI ◄ THROUGH PAMPLONA
◄ TO THE LONG WAIT AT SARAGOSSA ◄1◄ THENCE
RETURNING WITH THE HOSTAGE AL-ARABI WHO
WAS RETRIEVED BY HIS SONS ◄2◄ THE FRANKS
THEN BURN PAMPLONA ◄3◄ AND PROCEED TO
THE MOUNTAIN AMBUSH AT RONCEVAL WHERE
ROLAND DIED ◄4◄
AL-ARABI ◄
CHARLEMAGNE ◄
ALLIES FROM ◄ BAVARIA ◄ AUSTRIA ◄
PROVENCE ◄ LOMBARDY ◄
FRANKS AND ◄ ALLIES ◄

T. BOAK

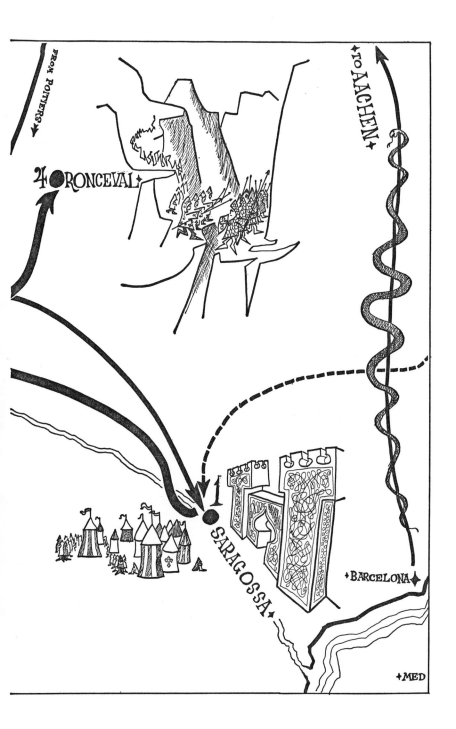

FROM POITIERS

TO AACHEN ✦

✦

4 ● RONCEVAL ✦

1 ● SARAGOSSA ✦

✦ BARCELONA ✦

✦ MED

READING
THE SONG OF
ROLAND

EUGENE VANCE

PRENTICE-HALL, INC., ENGLEWOOD CLIFFS, N.J.

Current printing (last number):

10 9 8 7 6 5 4 3 2 1

PRENTICE-HALL INTERNATIONAL, INC. (*London*)
PRENTICE-HALL OF AUSTRALIA, PTY. LTD. (*Sydney*)
PRENTICE-HALL OF CANADA, LTD. (*Toronto*)
PRENTICE-HALL OF INDIA PRIVATE LIMITED (*New Delhi*)
PRENTICE-HALL OF JAPAN, INC. (*Tokyo*)

ও§ PREFACE ৪৬

While writing this book I have tried to keep in mind the diversity of readers it will serve. However, I have found the task difficult of mediating between the needs of newcomers to French medieval poetry and of specialists. In so little space it is nearly impossible either to do justice to the corpus of established criticism or to introduce notions of my own in the manner that scholarship ordinarily demands. My goal as critic has been to bury polemics and to emphasize issues that I consider interesting and important, with the hope that the readers will follow up with investigations of their own. I have provided sufficient notes and appendices to guide any reader who wishes to deepen his response to the poem. I have also tried to raise questions about the *Song of Roland* that are pertinent to other epics and to the study of poetry as a whole. The *Song of Roland* reveals its true stature when studied comparatively.

I wish to express sincere thanks to several friends who have read the manuscript of this book at various stages: Miss Evelyn Birge, Mr. Michel-André Bossy, and Professor Christian Gellinek. Other friends, especially Professors Lee Patterson, Jeremy Adams, and Peter Haidu, have influenced me in important ways during long and congenial conversations about this and other medieval poems. Above all, I wish to express gratitude to Professor Maynard Mack who has corrected countless flaws of style and logic in my writing. It is a distinct privilege to benefit from the close criticisms of a scholar of such high standards, however unfulfilled such standards may remain in this book.

Much of this book was written during my tenure of a Morse Fellowship awarded to me by Yale University. I am deeply grateful to have been honored by such an opportunity.

EUGENE VANCE

◄§ CONTENTS §►

	INTRODUCTION	1
I.	THE STORY	4
II.	HEROIC CHARACTER AND ROLAND'S DISPUTE WITH GANELON	8
III.	FORMULAIC LANGUAGE AND HEROIC WARFARE	21
IV.	NARRATIVE SETTING AND THE LAISSE SIMILAIRE	39
V.	THE PASSION AND DEATH OF ROLAND	48
VI.	ROLAND, CHARLEMAGNE, AND TRAGIC PERSPECTIVE	64
VII.	THE BALIGANT EPISODE	72
VIII.	THE TRIAL AND PUNISHMENT OF GANELON: A CONCLUSION?	81

APPENDIX I: CHRONOLOGY — 94

APPENDIX II: THE HISTORICAL EVENT — 96

APPENDIX III: ROLAND AND THE CRITICS: A SYNOPSIS — 100

APPENDIX IV: FURTHER READING — 106

NOTES — 109

INDEX — 115

✑ INTRODUCTION ❧

As we read the *Song of Roland* for the first time, we quickly discover that its anonymous poet has left us a tale "which holdeth children from play and old men from the chimney corner," to use Sir Philip Sidney's phrase about how we should be affected by good heroic poetry. High-minded action and superhuman deeds secure our attention in a world where extremes of jubilance and despair, love and hatred, triumph and defeat, lay bare those ultimate boundaries of human potential which are for the most part hidden from our lives by the banality of everyday existence. Real life demands of us a thousand compromises a day, but the *Song of Roland,* like the *Iliad,* is a poem of absolutes. Its heroes commit sins, to be sure, but never sins of omission. This is an ethic of brutal pride, of high pulses and cut arteries, of *démesure.*

The solid core of action is probably what caused Roland's legend to become permanently embedded in the medieval imagination, to the point where he appeared in no less than forty other *chansons de geste* (epics) composed before 1400. Even during the renaissance this most medieval of heroes took a new lease on life as the florid hero of Italian epic-romances by Boiardo and Ariosto. For hundreds of years, then, the tale of Roland played on the European mind, engendering versions of itself both good and bad, but never losing prestige. What other legend (save those of Troy and Arthur of the Round Table) has reigned in the poetic imagination with such power as Roland's?

Modern readers of the *Song of Roland* will have no trouble responding to its high adventure for its own sake, and they may find that certain values which prevail in the poem—ideals such as loyalty, courage, honor, and strength—are still compatible with goals for which men struggle in our own century. At the same time, the sheer excitement of Roland's tale engages our minds in a world that is puzzlingly unlike our own. It is to be hoped that the uninitiated reader

1

will respond to this unfamiliar world with curiosity instead of dismay. Among my students both reactions have been common. After all, how should a reader react when he reads that Charlemagne, who is two hundred years old, tugs on his beard, and that twenty thousand Frenchmen faint to the ground when they learn that Roland is dead? Laugh? Weep? May we seriously hope to enlist a reader's enthusiasm for "sweet France" while Archbishop Turpin spreads a nationalized gospel of Christ (a poor man crucified among thieves) throughout Spain by hacking hundreds of Saracens apart with his sword? This kind of idea is odious nowadays (or is it?). Why should a reader finish a poem (many don't) if its principal hero (the only epic virgin from the *Iliad* to *Paradise Regained*) is already dead by the middle of the work? But then, who *is* the hero, anyway? Why in this story does the most powerful man in the world sit hanging his head and smoothing his moustache while his best leaders escalate a personal quarrel into an imperial catastrophe? How do we explain the lack of logic in the central conflicts which propel the poem's action; or the incredibly low verbal aptitude (to put it invidiously) of its heroes; or the poem's repetitiousness as countless swords split countless helmets, heads, and horses down the middle; or the tendency for the poet to narrate the same detail three times in a row? These are some of the peculiarities of the *Song of Roland* which test the manner in which we perceive the world against a framework of medieval attitudes about life and death.

Aside from its capacity to entertain us or to serve as an ethnological prism, the *Song of Roland* raises fascinating critical and interpretive problems which are relevant to the whole study of poetry as an art. May we speak of "unity" in a poem where the "unities" of time, place, and action are nonexistent? To what extent have we the right to subject a text reflecting a long background of oral improvisation to the procedures of close textual interpretation, justifiable within a tradition of "literary" poetry? What do the mysterious letters "AOI" that appear in the margin of the text signify? May we legitimately intellectualize about the material of a narrative poem not intellectually conceived by its author? Such problems tantalize the critic because they are always implicated in our appreciation of the poem, yet are finally unanswerable. These are questions which arise from within the poem; how many more questions arise from *without* the poem. Who wrote it? Where? When? Why? We do not know.

The purpose of this book is to encourage readers to recognize among the obscurities, the contradictions, and the improbable hyperboles of the *Song of Roland* a number of unmistakable triumphs which will make them eager to come to grips with the poem and its feudal world. Readers will perceive that the *Song of Roland* is not a simple poem, despite the austere directness of its style, and that the complexities it raises are perhaps relevant to those of our own age. Roland's fatal commitment to a chivalric ideal, for example, instills in us simultaneous feelings of awe and outrage; awe at the valor of Roland's choice to resist the Saracens unaided, outrage that his decision causes the destruction of all Charlemagne's most beloved vassals. Complex feelings of another kind are aroused in us by the episode of Ganelon's trial and punishment, where the poet probes the fundamental premises of order in feudal society by dramatizing the conflict between a vassal's obligation to his personal honor and to his lord. The *Song of Roland* is a moving poem, in that its poet has perceived the central problems of his age, yet he can guarantee no remedies, no alternatives, in his art. Like his characters, the poet of the *Song of Roland* has no vocabulary of compromise.

For those readers of the *Song of Roland* who will venture beyond modern English or French translations into the Old French text, some strong-blooded but accessible poetry stands ready to be explored. Midway between oral and written traditions of poetry, the *Song of Roland* is one of the earliest monuments of the French language; in the judgment of many, it is the single most important contribution of the medieval period to French poetry.

~§ I §~

THE STORY

Like so many masterpieces in our epic tradition, the *Song of Roland* begins by plunging us into the middle of a heroic world: Charlemagne and his army of knights have ravaged all Spain, and after seven long years only Saragossa, a mountain stronghold, remains uncaptured. Both the pagans and the French are exhausted with the war, and the pagans are holding council to devise a scheme that will induce the French to give up the siege and return to their homeland. We are already at a turning point in a tale of action, therefore, truly *in medias res*—the middle of the story where (in classical theory, at least) good epics are supposed to begin.

The Saracen council proposes the following plan: Blancandrin, one of King Marsile's chief barons, will journey to Charlemagne's court with twenty hostages and a promise that if Charlemagne returns to Aix (Aachen), Marsile will follow him there later and become his vassal. Marsile will promise exotic tribute to Charlemagne: bears, lions, hounds, camels, falcons, four hundred mules loaded with gold, and fifty wagonloads more of the same. Of course, the plan is that when Charlemagne leaves, the Saracens will renege, even though they know that their hostages will be put to death: pagan society is founded on treason.

Blancandrin arrives at Charlemagne's court and delivers Marsile's proposition. The French barons spontaneously mistrust the offer, and in Roland's first appearance he rises before the emperor and delivers an impassioned plea, straight from a heroic heart, that the French remain and wage war until vengeance is complete (XIV). While Charlemagne and the French brood in silence, Ganelon, Roland's stepfather, rises and vehemently denounces Roland's plea as counsel born of pride. When Ganelon recommends that Charlemagne accept Marsile as his vassal, the Duke of Naimes supports this strategy and the French peers are swayed to the wrong side (XVI).

4

Charlemagne requests an emissary to carry his response to Marsile. Everyone understands that this is a dangerous mission, because the last two emissaries (Basile and Basant) dispatched by Charlemagne to Marsile's court were put to death. Naimes, having supported the plan to negotiate, volunteers, but Charlemagne refuses to designate him because as one of Charlemagne's chief counselors he is too valuable to risk losing. When Roland proposes himself, Oliver quickly interjects that Roland is too proud and certainly would stir up trouble. After Charlemagne has refused other volunteers, Roland finally nominates Ganelon for the mission, and Ganelon explodes in wrath: Roland and his stepfather apparently share a long-standing enmity. Ganelon publicly threatens Roland and the twelve peers, and as Charlemagne invests Ganelon with the baton and the glove, symbols of authority, the glove ominously falls to the ground. Ganelon growls, "Lords, you will hear more of this!" (XXV).

Ganelon and Blancandrin start for Saragossa, and during the journey Ganelon persuades Blancandrin that the main obstacle to peace is Roland. When they arrive at Marsile's court, a stormy council ensues, during which Ganelon plans the following conspiracy with the pagan king: Ganelon will persuade Charlemagne to leave Spain and will arrange to have Roland designated leader of the French rearguard. When the French cross the Pyrenees, the pagans will ambush them and will exterminate Roland and the twelve peers. Ganelon returns to Charlemagne's court and falsely relates that the pagan army has drowned at sea, so that Charlemagne may return to Aix in peace. When Charlemagne requests a leader for the rearguard, Ganelon nominates Roland in full confidence that his honor will oblige him to accept (LVIII). Roland, in turn, receives the glove and the baton without letting either fall (LX). Despite his dreams prophesying a catastrophe at Ronceval, Charlemagne undertakes the journey back to France with his army. He weeps in advance of Roland's fate, and one hundred thousand soldiers echo his grief (LXVIII).

With Roland chief of the rearguard, the French begin their trek across the mountains. Roland and Oliver hear the pagans approaching before they attack, and an argument erupts between the two Frenchmen about what they should do. Oliver urges Roland to sound his horn and summon help from Charlemagne, but Roland refuses because he regards the forthcoming conflict as another test of his heroic honor (LXXXVII). Archbishop Turpin promises absolution and salvation to anyone martyred in battle (XC). The war against the pagans begins as Roland strikes the initial blow: primacy in the epic world is a mark of prestige. The peers each follow suit with mighty blows of their own, and the Christians exult in their deeds of prowess until the pagans begin to turn the tide of battle against them (CXVI). When Roland pauses long enough to see that his best men are being slaughtered, he asks Oliver for advice (CXXVIII). A new quarrel breaks out between them when Roland declares that he will sound his horn after all. Oliver sees Roland's decision as a lapse of honor (CXXX), but Turpin defends it by pointing out that the horn cannot possibly bring rescue, only vengeance (CXXXII). Roland finally sounds his Oliphant and Charlemagne intuitively understands the nature of the calamity at hand. He arrests Ganelon and has him tortured by scullery serfs (CXXXVII).

Roland, meanwhile, looks about him and laments the loss of his barons (CXL). He rallies from despair, however, and leads his men to renew their heroic deeds. Soon Oliver is fatally wounded and calls out to his companion for help. As Roland approaches, Oliver mistakes him for a Saracen and, courageous even in blindness, strikes Roland with his sword (CXLIX). When Roland asks why Oliver has struck him, Oliver recognizes his error and the friends forgive each other and embrace in love; then Oliver dies (CLI). Roland rejoins the battle, but soon withdraws to gather up the bodies of his dead companions to mourn their loss. As Roland himself nears death, he climbs a hill and collapses. A pagan tries to steal his sword, but Roland kills him with a blow from his Oliphant (CLXX). In order to keep his sword from falling into a coward's hands, Roland tries to break it on a stone (CLXXII). Astonished by his sword's indestructibility, Roland delivers a moving soliloquy and dies a conqueror still facing his enemy (CLXXIV). Angels descend and bear his soul up to heaven.

Charlemagne returns to Ronceval and wreaks vengeance upon the pagan army by driving them into the river Ebro (CLXXX). Meanwhile, a new, more powerful Moslem chief arrives in Spain to rescue the pagan cause (CXC). Before Charlemagne engages in a new battle, he returns to Ronceval to recover Roland's body. He finds Roland lying with his face directed defiantly toward Spain and delivers a long monologue in which he grieves, not only for the personal loss of his favorite nephew, but for the destruction of his empire as well (CCVII). The ten battle-corps of the French and the thirty of the pagans engage in a new war, whose climax is a duel between Charlemagne and Baligant. God intervenes just before Baligant's sword bites into Charlemagne's brain, and Charlemagne returns a blow that strikes Baligant dead (CCLXII).

The battle over, Charlemagne returns to Aix and prosecutes Ganelon for treason. Ganelon defends his acts, claiming that he had conspired with Marsile for the sake of *private* vengeance, but that he had not betrayed his lord (CCLXXIII). A vassal named Pinabel offers himself as Ganelon's champion in a judicial duel, and he is answered by Thierry, who speaks for the emperor's cause: Roland was in Charlemagne's service, and by attacking Roland, Ganelon compromised the interests of his lord (CCLXXVII). The duel that ensues concludes when God intercepts a blow by Pinabel the instant before it reaches Thierry's skull. Thierry returns the blow and falls Pinabel. God has shown his will and Ganelon now must die. Selecting a punishment to fit the crime, the barons decide to quarter Ganelon instead of hanging him. They tie him to four horses, and he is torn to pieces. Charlemagne allows Bramimond, Marsile's wife, to be baptized as a Christian. The poem concludes as the angel Gabriel visits Charlemagne in a dream and summons him once again to take up arms in the service of God. Charlemagne tugs at his beard and weeps. "Here ends the *geste* that Turold has compiled."

✣ II ✣

HEROIC CHARACTER AND

ROLAND'S DISPUTE

WITH GANELON

The *Song of Roland* is a poem of violent passions. All epic heroes are perhaps passionate men by nature, but the attitudes of various poets in the epic tradition toward passion differ widely. In Homer, the wrath of Achilles was a glorious but finally degrading force; in Virgil, wrath and desire impeded the birth of empires. In the Christian ethic, founded upon the agony of a man-god nailed upon a cross, passion (and also *com*passion) assumed a vital role in the drama of self-fulfillment and salvation.[1] Although passion propels the action of medieval Christian literature of all genres, from Saint Augustine's *Confessions* to Dante's *Divine Comedy,* no medieval hero can quite match the gusty, full-blown emotionality of Roland and his peers in this first masterpiece of French poetry.

Strong and clear though the outlines of human character seem in this poem, the question of how these characters found their way into the narrative is complicated and poorly understood. Most scholars now believe that the story of Roland, whether in the form of poem or legend (or both), passed through many stages of development before it achieved the form we know today in the so-called "Oxford" version of the poem.

In its earliest form, the *Song of Roland* may have originated at the time of the catastrophe at Ronceval itself, and may conceivably have narrated the ambush of Charlemagne's rearguard the way it actually happened. Subsequently, so the theory goes, generations of *jongleurs* (wandering, oral poets) added new material to that nucleus of history, expanding it here and there and adding characters as they were needed to make the story timely and entertaining. Thus, a tale that perhaps first celebrated Roland's deeds at Ronceval attracted a "legion" of anonymous, oral poets through the ages and remained in more or less constant revision for three centuries after the event itself, when some poet of genius imposed upon his inherited material a triumphant form, which inspired some scribe to set the poem down upon parchment. Some critics believe that the name "Turold" in the poem's final verse is that of the poet; others believe that "Turold" was only the scribe.

Those critics who are convinced of the historical veracity of the *Song of Roland* believe that the deeds of Roland in 778 constituted a primitive narrative framework for the poem. Ganelon may have made his way into the poem as early as the ninth century. Oliver, by contrast, seems to have appeared sometime during the tenth century, apparently the contribution of some poet whose intention was to inject a new moral element into an old poetic legend. In short, scholars holding these theories believe that they can detect "layers" of history in the poem.

The case for Oliver's appearance at a later phase of the poem's development rests on some interesting external evidence. A number of scholars have noticed that starting in the first half of the eleventh century, the name "Oliver" (*Olivarius* or *Oliverius*) begins to occur in documents in France, Spain, and Italy and in frequent conjunction with the name "Roland." Apparently, some widespread vogue during the eleventh century caused fathers to name their sons consecutively after the two heroes. This evidence supports our belief that oral versions of the *Song of Roland* circulated around Europe well before the Oxford version was set down on parchment at the end of the eleventh century.[2]

The twelve peers in the poem whom Charlemagne summons to his council are with one possible exception either fictitious or else historically anachronistic with the event of 778; this same a-historicity is true of the majority of the fifty-six Christians named in the poem.[3] As for the peers' number, twelve, critics have suggested on the one hand that it is in accord with the custom of feudal lords in northern France to summon their twelve principal vassals to sit for judicial matters, and on the other hand, that the council is a figurative representation of the twelve apostles of Christ. We need not see here any contradiction.[4] Other critics suspect a connection between the twelve peers and the knights of Arthur's Round Table.[5]

My purpose here is not to recapitulate or judge the different theories of origins that have been brought to bear upon the *Song of Roland*. It should be clear, though, that the poet drew his material indiscriminately from history, from poetic legend, and from what the poet *thought* was history. The diversity of such sources ought to discourage us from presuming that there is any clear-cut logical sequence of phenomena leading from the historical to the literary event. For the moment, we should emphasize only that the story of Ronceval was the legacy of a very long narrative tradition and that the poet inherited characters whose literary personalities were somewhat predetermined. Thus, the relationships between Charlemagne, Roland, Oliver, and Ganelon formed an inviolable skeleton already well known to the audience. Indeed, the audience's familiarity with such material would have enhanced their willingness to listen. In an oral epic whose plot and characters are already known by heart and sanctified by tradition, there can be few mysteries and few surprises; the talent of the individual poet will tend to make itself felt in the beauty and skill of the poem's execution rather than in experimental innovations.

Such arguments should not discourage the reader from seeking reasons intrinsic to the poem itself to account for its persons, episodes, or scenes. It seems obvious to me that at some moment a single, controlling artistic spirit imposed itself upon these traditional sources and mastered them. Some poet with a deep understanding of his inherited material fashioned a work of art that is eclectic but coherent and intelligible in its own terms.

Sure of his audience's expectations, the poet of the *Song of Roland* introduces his principal characters (except Charlemagne) only after their setting has been well prepared. When in *laisse* XII he does present them, they appear in a cluster and with epithets which predetermine and prejudge their identities:

> Along with the others came Count Roland,
> And Oliver, one bold, the other noble;
> There were more than a thousand Francs;
> Ganelon came, he who committed treason.
> Now begins the council which brought evil.[6] (XII)

Obviously, characters already describable in such terms bring into the poem with them a basic framework of causality from which the action must derive. The mere mention of their names together is evidently enough by this time to guarantee a tale of tragedy, a tragedy complete in the minds of both poet and audience before it even "happens."

Like the characters of the *Iliad,* then, the characters of the *Song of Roland* enter the poem with an established identity. In contrast with the hero of modern literature, such as Hamlet, Alyosha Karamazov, or Paul Morel, the hero of French epic does not discover the meaning of life by creating his own role in the world; rather, he enters a world of fixed truths with a fixed identity to be tested by the spears and swords of outrageous Fortune. In other words, the unfolding of time in the *Song of Roland* does not bring progressive states of awareness in its hero; it measures instead human *constancy* and not *change.* Roland does not grow qualitatively during his ordeals, but only becomes more like himself as the tale advances. Compared to a courtly *roman d'aventure* such as Chretien de Troyes' *Perceval* (ca. 1179) where the word *aventure* implies a true psychological futurity for the characters, the *Song of Roland* deals only with characters who are "presences." Moreover, the "futurity" of the Roland story itself is only a tenuous fiction ready to be dispensed with by the poet at any time— even his characters fore-know every major event in the poem. The organizing perspective of time, like the perspective of space for painters, does not characterize early Romanesque art.

When Charlemagne reveals King Marsile's proposition to the council of French barons—namely, that if Charlemagne, in exchange for hostages and great treasures, will return to Aix, Marsile will follow him there, accept baptism, and become his vassal—we of the audience already know the motivation behind this proposition and have a privileged vantage point from which to examine the responses of the various Frenchmen. The barons spontaneously exclaim, "Watch out!" and we know that their primary instincts as pious Christians are reliable. Roland seconds their sentiments by reminding Charlemagne of an earlier, ill-fated embassy, when Basile and Basant were sent to a Saracen court and were put to death.

It would seem, at first, as though the poet were caught up in the clichés of piety of his crusading age ("The pagans are all wrong and the Christians right!").[7] It soon becomes clear, however, that the poet is not complacent about the broad moral prejudices that govern his treatment of Saracen and Christian societies. To be sure, Roland is strategically justified in his counsel that Charlemagne reject any negotiation with the pagans; but there are signs of extremism in his

attitude which cause us to suspect that he is right for the wrong reasons. He is too anxious to recite his own conquests to convince us that
he is not motivated by vainglory. Roland's heady advice to the two-
hundred-year-old Charlemagne that he undertake a siege of revenge
even if it takes a lifetime, leaves little doubt that Roland's strategic
outlook stems largely from an excess of heroic pride.

Charlemagne's reactions lend strength to our suspicion. Though he
himself has a long past of military glory and is only too familiar with
the thirst for fame that spurs a heroic temperament, he is by now a
Roland grown wiser, a tired man who has seen beyond the glories of
chivalric heroism. Consanguinity in medieval and renaissance literature
usually implies a common identity between people; yet consanguinity
can also dramatize contrary aspects of a single ideal. In the nephew-
uncle relationship of Roland and Charlemagne we find two contrasting
perspectives upon the cult of chivalric heroism. Thus, when Roland
uncorks his pride before the council, Charlemagne broods in painful
silence. Everyone, in fact, is hushed at Roland's display of zeal:

> The emperor sits with his head cast down.
> He smooths his beard and straightens his moustache,
> Without answering his nephew good or bad;
> The Frenchmen all are silent. . . . (XV)

Do Charlemagne and the French barons balk at Roland's challenge out
of embarrassment? Humiliation? Fear? The exact meaning behind
Charlemagne's emblematic gestures remains concealed, yet they suggest that this silence is pregnant with events that will rend the very
soul of the heroic world.

Most striking is that Charlemagne, master of the world and vicar of
Christ on earth, should appear so passive before the impetuous advice of a vassal who, after all, is very much his inferior. We may choose
any of several explanations for this. In the first place, Charlemagne is
obligated as a feudal lord to listen to the counsel of his vassals, just as
they are obligated to give it—indeed, these are problems of leadership
in any age. Second, it might be argued that Charlemagne and his barons
emanate from a world dominated by a sense of predestination against
which any struggle would be futile. A third and more likely explanation lies in the pervasive attitude in the *Song of Roland* that human
character—especially heroic character—is basically unchangeable. Not
only do the poet and the audience know that the characters in this

legend are tempered by time in their traditional ways, but the characters *themselves* seem to know it. Charlemagne's impotence is a kind of hyperbole: the strongest man in the world is helpless before the miracle of human nature. Tragedy must have its way.

The Frenchmen's worst fears materialize as Ganelon breaks the silence and abusively expresses what others perhaps already feel about Roland. In the ethos of the *Song of Roland,* where discourse is never detached from the realm of physical action, a verbal quarrel inevitably issues in an event; we sense in the dispute between Roland and Ganelon the first phase of a violent tragedy which is pressing to happen. Ganelon, as noted above, is Roland's stepfather—this is the reverse of relationship by consanguinity and stresses how intimate the antipathy between Roland and Ganelon is. Ganelon is a formidable rival who will seize any opportunity to degrade Roland before his peers. First he attacks Roland's mania for combat, and then he offers a counterproposal:

> Ganelon leaps to his feet before Charles,
> With great pride he begins his argument
> And says to the King, "Never trust a fool,
> Me or any other disloyal to your cause.
> When Marsile asks to swear an oath of homage,
> And with hands clasped to become your vassal,
> And by your grace to hold the whole of Spain
> And to submit to laws that we observe—
> Whoever says we should reject this plea
> Does not care if we live or die.
> A counsel born of pride must not be heard.
> Forget the fools; let's stick with the wise men." (XV)

The moral dilemma has now become doubly paradoxical: Roland was strategically right for the wrong reason; now Ganelon is strategically wrong for the *right* reasons! In less than 250 lines the poet has sketched a complicated political dispute whose structure depends upon lines of love and hatred existing between the characters themselves. Destiny is commensurate with human character in this poem, so that free will remains intact as characters draw each other into a tragedy that is both inevitable and chosen.

The French council resolves to follow Ganelon's arguments instead of Roland's and to send an emissary to the Saracen court. Charlemagne, however, can bring himself neither to designate an emissary nor to accept a volunteer because he is too deeply attached to his men. From his paroxysms of rage at different proposals, we sense that the situation is beyond his control. First the Duke of Naimes and then Roland offer themselves for the post. It has been suggested that Roland knows in advance that he is unacceptable—after all, he is one of the twelve peers and nephew of Charlemagne himself—and that he is manipulating himself into a position where he can nominate Ganelon. This is out of character, however. Roland is basically uncomplicated and monolithic throughout his epic, and is spurred here as elsewhere by a passionate desire to assay his courage. By offering to go on a mission that he knows will endanger his life, Roland effectively converts a question of political strategy into a question of personal honor, and it will henceforth be impossible for the French barons to consider the issue in any other light. The omniscient reader can only be aware of the discrepancy between strategy and honor, a discrepancy, we may be sure, that all too often eludes leaders of our own violent times.

Oliver, who has been silent until now, angrily interrupts Roland's offer to serve as Charlemagne's envoy and scolds Roland as only a hero's best friend could: "Certainly, you'll not go . . . your heart is harsh and proud; I fear you'll stir up trouble" (XVIII). Though uttered in loyalty and not hatred, Oliver's criticism of Roland's character is similar to Ganelon's, in that both agree that he is proud. The only difference lies in their vocabulary, for Ganelon accuses Roland of *orguill* (equivalent to the Latin *superbia*), and Oliver criticizes him with the more flattering word, *fiers.*

Oliver is trenchant in his assessment of Roland's character, but at the same time Oliver characterizes himself as well. He knows that Roland's hot-headed courage is potentially destructive, and his discreeter nature leads him to try to temper that impulsiveness. Oliver is *sage.* As Patroclus to Achilles, Oliver is devoted to Roland and will pay with his life for it.

For all his rectitude, Oliver is never granted the slightest power to affect the direction of events in the poem. Deprived of this highest dignity in a poem of action, Oliver plays only an ancillary part to Roland. The limited nature of Oliver's role has encouraged critics to believe that he was added late in the tale's development by some poet who wanted Roland and Oliver to exemplify the complementary virtues of *fortitudo* and *sapientia,* which since classical times had constituted the twin virtues of the ideal warrior:

> Roland is bold and Oliver is wise.
> Together they make excellent vassals. . . . (LXXXVII)

These critics point out that Oliver's name is the only one in the poem deriving from Latin, that the olive tree and its oil could symbolize peace and wisdom, and that Oliver as a character enters the poem with no historical pedigree attached to his name.[8] Certainly, the association between the olive branch and the idea of peace is warranted by the poem (V, VI, VII, XIV), but the occasional opposition between Oliver the "wise" and Roland the "bold" is undercut by the fact that elsewhere in the poem these words are used indiscriminately as stock epithets for Christians and pagans. My view is that Oliver is conceived more as person than as idea. Nevertheless, we may perhaps detect two historical layers of the poem here, which add in the upshot to its interest and complexity.

Sensing the mounting danger, Archbishop Turpin tries to settle the problem of selecting an envoy by offering himself. Being a good medieval bishop, Turpin does not like to see division among Christ's vassals. He will have occasion to mediate again in another quarrel between Roland and Oliver (CXXXII). Turpin asks Charlemagne for the baton and glove, symbols of the embassy, for himself. By now the reader may have noticed that the poet marks a rhythm in the narrative as the quarrel between Roland and Ganelon becomes more generalized: with each aggravation a more important figure (Naimes twice, Oliver once, and finally Turpin) intervenes and tries to deflect the course of events away from that disaster that the conflict must inevitably bring. In his helplessness, Charlemagne only becomes more irascible: "Go sit down on your white rug! Don't say anything unless I command it!" (XIX).

There is a point, however, beyond which the pressure of violence cannot be restrained. When Turpin's offer to serve as ambassador is rejected, Charlemagne makes his fateful request a third and final time: "Noble knights, select a baron from my lands to carry a message to Marsile." Roland and Ganelon, who so far have not spoken directly to each other, are close to bursting out in flames of open argument. Now the answer comes to Charlemagne's question, an answer that will have dreadful consequences for all: Roland says, "It will be Ganelon, my stepfather" (XX).

What immediately follows in the Oxford version of the *Song of Ro-*

land has caused a vast polemic among commentators on the poem, and
it typifies the kind of textual crux that often confronts medievalists.
In the Oxford version, the sequence of events is as follows: Roland
designates Ganelon for the embassy. The French barons, who evidently
see no other recourse, approve the choice. Pierced with anguish, Ganelon rises, throws off his cloak in wrath, and addresses Roland: "Completely mad! Why such rage? Everyone knows very well that I am your
stepfather, and now you choose me to go to Marsile!" He then growls
out a personal threat, which Roland matches by insolent mockery and
an offer to go in his place (XX). The offer is made as a gratuitous jibe,
of course, because Roland knows that the mission has already been
denied him. He knows, too, that even if it were not, Ganelon could
not accept him as a substitute without losing his honor. Ganelon
spurns Roland's offer and reiterates his threat of revenge, this time
allowing his hatred to vent itself unmistakably:

> "I will go to Saragossa and Marsile.
> But I will take revenge on you some day
> Before I calm this mighty wrath of mine." (XXI)

At this, Roland laughs.

Ganelon's anger spreads in widening circles. At first, Roland was its
sole object; now it includes Oliver and the twelve peers. After a time,
however, it burns less hotly and Ganelon recovers his dignity. He presents himself to Charlemagne, commends to him his son, and receives
Charlemagne's official designation as ambassador to Marsile's court
(XXIII). Next he takes up the baton and glove, which are symbols of
his mission, and swears an oath of vengeance on Roland, Oliver, and
the twelve peers (XXIV). When he drops the glove that Charlemagne
has given him, it is a clear omen of some sinister event in the offering.
Ganelon's men weep as he withdraws to undertake the journey with
Blancandrin (XXVII). Critics have noticed that in all the other versions
and fragments of the *Roland,* the order of details is different. There the
sequence is as follows. First, Charles asks his fatal question, and Roland
designates Ganelon. The choice is thereupon *immediately* ratified by
Charles, and Ganelon presents himself to the emperor and consents to
do his duty. Ganelon then commends his son to Charlemagne. Next,
he rises, takes off his cloak, and lashes out at Roland, as in the Oxford
manuscript, with a threat. Roland offers himself as a substitute for
Ganelon. Ganelon disdains the offer, as his honor demands, but threat-

ens to do Roland an evil deed before returning—until then his wrath cannot be appeased. Roland laughs. Ganelon feels "great anguish" and formally repudiates his friendship with Roland, Oliver, and the twelve peers. Then he goes forward to accept the baton and glove, which he lets fall, as in the Oxford manuscript.

The assumption among certain critics, based on arguments too complicated to repeat here, is that the order of details in the other versions of the *Song of Roland* is more authentic than that in the Oxford version because it is clearer and more harmonious, hence more "natural." [9] True, the Oxford version presents some apparent contradictions: for example, before Charlemagne has spoken a single word about Ganelon's mission, Ganelon says, "Charles orders me to serve him: I will go to Marsile at Saragossa" (XXI). True, too, the more recent versions of the poem postulate a much more reasoned sequence of events.[10] Those who defend the Oxford version point out that if the barons unanimously approve Ganelon's designation, then consent by Charlemagne may be taken for granted. However, one may be less legalistic and add that the earlier poet is not meticulous about the chronology of his narrative, and that it is in the tempestuous nature of his characters to ignore the restraints of protocol and to allow their passions to be triggered at the slightest provocation to their honor. In the later versions, Ganelon feels his "anguish" only after Charlemagne has formally appointed him to the mission and only after Roland has impudently laughed at him. By contrast, the earlier poet *starts* by telling of the "anguish" of Ganelon, and *then* he confirms its cause. The earlier poem gives, thereby, an impression of awesome spontaneity as characters are transported by rage; the later poems convey a sense of homogeneity and aesthetic distance between the poet and his characters.[11]

One of the main differences between the early and later versions of the *Song of Roland,* then, is that chronology has gained authority in its own right: the later poets tend to see human experience as unfolding in a framework of time.[12] This intellectual habit is a contribution of the later middle ages and has dominated narrative, with exceptions, until the early decades of our own century. The early *Song of Roland,* though, thrives on anachronisms. Ganelon's men weep for him even before he departs for Marsile's court; Charlemagne weeps as Roland accepts his charge as head of the rearguard; the sun is mysteriously eclipsed before a hair of Roland's head has been harmed. The poet of the Oxford manuscript is constantly anticipating the outcome of his own story, both in Charlemagne's prophetic dreams and in outright statements of what is to come, such as the following:

> The battle, meanwhile, turned more violent;
> Both French and pagans gave marvelous blows.
> Some strike out, while others defend themselves.
> So many spears broken and bloodied!
> So many gallant Frenchmen lose their youth!
> Nor will they see their wives and mothers again,
> Nor the people of France who wait at home.
> Charles the Great weeps and laments for them all.
> But what good? There will be no rescue.
> Ganelon served him an evil turn that day
> When he sold himself out in Saragossa.
> Because of this he lost both life and limb;
> At his trial in Aix he was sentenced to hang,
> Along with thirty of his relatives
> Who did not expect to die this way. (CIX)

If Ganelon explodes in the council before Charlemagne has appointed him to the embassy, this is primarily because Ganelon and Roland are involved in a demonic process whose mainspring is their pride and their mortal hatred for each other. Ganelon is as proud as Roland; he knows that he cannot back down honorably and must endorse his advice to Charlemagne with his own person. But Ganelon will have his moment of revenge later, and his success will depend entirely on his complete assurance that he will be able to maneuver Roland into accepting leadership of the rearguard. When Charlemagne asks the fatal question, Ganelon will say, "Let it be Roland, my stepson." This *laisse* will have the same assonance as that in which Roland names Ganelon. Their proclamations will contain an identical number of syllables, and Roland will leap up in anguish, as Ganelon did earlier, well before Charlemagne has ratified the choice. To the last detail, revenge in this poem is symmetrical.

When Ganelon steps forward to accept the glove and baton from Charles, and the glove falls to the ground, the worst suspicions of the Frenchmen are aroused: "Lord! What could this mean?" Does Ganelon drop the glove intentionally, or does it drop by accident? The ambiguity is intriguing because it invites us to consider the forthcoming tragedy both as the visitation of an evil destiny and as the consequence of malevolent pride. The poet is not willing to distinguish between interior and exterior causality in the actions of his characters. Here, as elsewhere in the *Song of Roland,* interventions of supernatural forces in the action do not violate human intentions; on the contrary, they bear out and amplify tendencies already implicit in the characters themselves. The self-determining qualities of the human will always remain in the foreground of the *Song of Roland*; and as far as we are concerned, we do not have to decide whether Ganelon dropped the glove or whether it fell. "Lords," he says, "you'll hear more news of this!"

The extent to which the design of the *Song of Roland* is contingent upon traits of human character (which may simultaneously be viewed as aspects of destiny) becomes more apparent as Ganelon plots his treason with Blancandrin during their journey to Marsile's court. The first step in his plan for revenge is to persuade Blancandrin that the real cause of Charlemagne's hostilities in Spain is Roland, whom he accuses of aspiring to conquer all peoples: "When someone kills Roland, then we will have peace" (XXIX). Naturally, Ganelon's plan to maneuver Roland into command of the rearguard will require some arranging, since Roland and the twelve peers habitually take charge of the van. Ganelon, however, never doubts for a moment that Roland will respond to the challenge to his honor which Ganelon means to issue when he returns from Saragossa. Ganelon has risked *his* life in the embassy to Marsile; once back with Charlemagne, he can challenge Roland to undertake the risk of commanding the rearguard. Roland's pride will force him to accept the command. Honor dictates the forward motion of the poem.

The *Song of Roland* is an exalted stylization of the realities of the feudal world. Distortion is an important component of technique in romanesque art—in sculpture as well as in poetry—and in this poem it serves to abolish the greys of ordinary life and to situate human beings in an idealized sphere which is morally black and white.[13] The eleventh-century audience is invited to look beyond the confusions of everyday life into a world of timeless heroes. The poet protects the character of that world for them by allowing into it nothing that is not extraordinary or monumental. Yet the artificiality of the *Song of Roland* encourages no moral escapism; on the contrary, it abjures the paleness of day-to-day banalities for acts that are purer, more violent, and bigger than life, acts that demand, as medieval codes at their best always do, not less than everything a human being can offer. This deliberate withdrawal from the commonplace is characteristic of all epic and heroic poetry. As we shall see in the following chapter, what distinguishes the *Song of Roland* from other epics is the degree to which the poet depends upon raw hyperboles of force and unrefined violence to guarantee the challenge of his fictional world to all forms of mediocrity and easy compromise.

‎☙ III ❧

FORMULAIC LANGUAGE AND

HEROIC WARFARE

The manuscript of the Oxford version of the *Song of Roland* was produced by an Anglo-Norman scribe sometime during the third quarter of the twelfth century. Its language is basically the dialect spoken in England a century after the Norman conquest (1066);[1] but the actual poem on which the Oxford manuscript is based predates this manuscript by at least a half century, and we cannot be certain whether the poet lived in England or on the continent.

A reader who has even a scant knowledge of French will recognize after brief exposure to the *Song of Roland* that its poetic idiom relies on movable clusters of words, which we arbitrarily call "formulas." All language, even the most neutral prose, is to some extent formulaic; but in an oral tradition from which poems like the *Iliad* and the *Song of Roland* emerge, the use of formulaic language is a highly developed technique of composition. During the last few decades scholars have paid much attention to bards of rural Yugoslavia who still perpetuate an ancient narrative tradition and who are capable of reciting long epics from memory; as a result, we know that oral technique poses special problems for the literary critic.

Though there are many metrical irregularities in the Oxford manuscript, the standard line in the *Song of Roland* is assonanced and has ten syllables with a caesura after the fourth syllable. Any regular line in the poem will therefore call for the following components: one verbal unit of four syllables, another of six syllables, and a terminal vowel sound which fulfills the assonance of the *laisse*:

> 1 2 3 4   5 6 7 8 9 10
> Carles le reis, // nostre emperere magnes,
>
> 1 2 3 4   5 6 7 8 9 10
> Set anz tuz pleins // ad estet en Espaigne:
>
> 1 2 3 4   5 6 7 8 9 10
> Tresqu'en la mer // cunquist la tere altaigne . . . I

Because an oral poet tended to improvise during the recitation of his poem, he would draw on a stockpile of memorized formulas to satisfy the demands of meter and assonance that characterised his narrative form. Doubtless, the melodic accompaniment to his narrative was also composed of formulas and variations. It is not easy to define a "formula" in oral poetry. An oral formula has frequently been described by students of the epic as "a group of words which is regularly employed under the same metrical conditions to express a given, essential idea." [2] However, the *Song of Roland* is full of formulas that may be inflected to suit all kinds of metrical conditions and may be contracted to a single hemistiche or expanded to occupy an entire *laisse*. Formulas tend to unite identifiable clusters of words which convey a particular idea, but the basis of a formula is not exclusively verbal. I am convinced that a formula may also exist in the memory as a non-verbal *Gestalt* before it is clothed in words that satisfy the metrical demands of the Old French decasyllabic verse. Whatever cognitive process underlies formulaic technique, this technique allowed a *jongleur* to compose without weighing his diction and to embellish his traditional themes by exploiting a "ragbag" of well-tried expressions that were the basic implements of his trade and the common property of all.

The tradition of epic poetry in northern France served the interests of a *de facto* aristocracy, which first began to establish itself by courage and military power following the disintegration of the Carolingian Empire. By the year A.D. 1000, political power had become so dispersed that the State for all practical purposes no longer existed, and the only real political unit was the fortified castle of a small lord who could offer protection to a certain number of local dependents attached to his domain.[3] In this emerging military caste, the knight remained the nobleman *par excellence,* and the language of oral epic poetry which evolved during this period of French history favored the military values of that ruling caste. Consequently, the poetic language of the Old French epic was better able to deal literally with the action of warfare than with any other sector of human experience. Hence, when the poet of the *Song of Roland* describes the war between Christians and pagans, he unfolds a dowry of traditional formulas which represent in codified form the heroic ideals of a ruling chivalric class. If the *Song of Roland* is socially exclusive—the lower orders of society have no place in the poem—the poem's formulaic language is also exclusive and posits what amounts to a utopia of chivalric values, an idealized and simplified world where the nobility could find delivery from the torpor of everyday life and fulfill their most ardent dreams.

Because warfare was the primary activity of the early feudal nobility, it is no surprise that scenes depicting the key moments of combat rely more heavily upon traditional formulas than passages dealing with less typical areas of feudal life.[4] Even though some readers may not be able to read the passages below with ease, they will recognize, through the recurrence of certain patterns of word and idea, that the poet operates within a well-defined system of formulas. The Old French epic formula is not like the Old English "kenning" (which occurs, for instance, when the poet of *Beowulf* calls the sea a "whale-road") or those Homeric formulas that have a decorative allure ("the wine-dark sea"). On the contrary, it usually contains a "unit" of action, a single gesture, which combines with other formulas to generate a descriptive whole. As examples I have chosen several episodes in which a Christian slays a Saracen with his sword. Though the descriptions are enriched with variations, the poet is obviously following a single basic procedure as he presents that moment when a Christian's sword splits a pagan down the middle. I have purposely made my translations here as literal as possible, at the expense of meter, logic, and even syntax:

> Trait Durendal, sa bone espee, nue,
> Sun cheval brochet, si vait ferir Chernuble.
> L'elme li freint u li carbuncle luisent,
> Trenchent le cors [?] e la cheveleüre,
> Si li trenchat les oilz e la faiture,
> Le blanc osberc, dunt la maile est menue,
> E tut le cors tresqu'en la furcheüre.
> Enz en la sele, ki est a or batue,
> El cheval est l'espee aresteüe;
> Trenchet l'eschine, hunc n'i out quis jointure.
> Tut abat mort el pred sur l'erbe drue. (CIV)

> He draws Durendal, his good sword, bare;
> He spurs his horse, and goes to strike Chernuble.
> He smashes his helmet where the carbuncles shine,
> He splits the body and the hair on his head,
> He splits the eyes and the face,
> The white mail, whose chain is fine,
> And the whole body right down to the crotch.

Into the saddle, which is of beaten gold,
Into the horse the sword went and stopped;
It splits the spine without seeking the joint,
And slaughters him dead on the field of thick grass.

In a less expansive version, where Oliver strikes the pagan Justin de Val Ferree, we still see the same motifs:

Danz Oliver trait ad sa bone espee
Que ses cumpainz Rollant li ad tant demandee,
E li il ad cum chevaler mustree.
Fiert un paier., Justin de Val Ferree.
Tute la teste li ad par mi sevree,
Trenchet le cors et la bronie safree,
La bone sele, ki a or est gemmee,
E al ceval a l'eschine trenchee:
Tut abat mort devant loi en la pree. (CVII)

Lord Oliver has drawn his good sword
As his companion Roland has so long asked,
And he shows it off as befits a knight.
He strikes a pagan, Justin de Val Ferree.
He severed the whole head down the middle,
He splits the body and the saffron mail,
The good saddle, which is in gemmed gold,
And splits the horse through the spine:
He slaughters him dead before him in the field.

Here again is how Roland slays Grandonie:

Li quens le fiert tant vertuusement
Tresqu'al nasei tut le elme li fent,
Trenchet le nés e la buche e les denz,
Trestut le cors e l'osberc jazerenc,
De l'oree sele lé dous alves d'argent
E al ceval le dos parfundement;
Ambure ocist seinz nul recoevrement
E cil d'Espaigne s'en cleiment tuit dolent. (CXXIV)

The count strikes him with such power
On the noseguard that he cracks the whole helmet.
He splits the nose and the mouth and the teeth,
Through the whole body and the linked mail,
And the pummel and the silver cantle

> And deeply into the horse's back;
> He kills them both beyond all reprieve,
> And those from Spain cry out in anguish.

Such is the manner in which the epic hero, be it Roland, Oliver, or any other, slaughters a Saracen in single-handed combat. The force and precision with which a knight splits a pagan in two (and his horse) are the basis for honor and esteem in this chivalric world. As Roland cries out to Oliver during battle,

> "Now I know you, brother!
> If the emperor loves us, it's for such blows!"
> From every side the cry "Munjoie!" resounds. (CVII)'

The reader will notice that all the distinct phases of chivalric combat entail their characteristic formulas—the taking up of arms, the mobilization of the army, the assault against the masses by a single-handed hero, the moment of the lance's impact—and that these formulas comprise the raw material from which countless scenes and episodes will be built. These formulas enter the poem with a built-in ethical value, and we may say of our poet's language what one critic has said of Homer's: "The formulaic character of Homer's language means that everything in the world is regularly presented as all men (all men within the poem, that is) commonly perceive it. The style of Homer emphasizes constantly the accepted attitude toward each thing in the world, and this makes for a great unity of experience." [5] This "unity of experience," which is a function of the conventionality in the poem's language, would seem to create difficulties for a poet who wishes to isolate what is *particular* about a given individual; yet he may overcome this dilemma by making *quantitative,* rather than *qualitative,* distinctions between his characters' actions. Fatally wounded, for example, Archbishop Turpin delivers more than a thousand blows (CLIV); Roland puts a whole army to rout (CLX). In other words, the poet of the *Song of Roland* distinguishes his heroes by magnifying them, just as a romanesque sculptor (such as the master of Vézelay) will make his Christ twice as big as the lesser spiritual heroes around him. Physical dimensions and God-given force are measures of spiritual virtue in twelfth-century art.

As the story of Roland passed beyond the tenth century, certain tensions inevitably developed in a heroic ideal that was becoming increasingly archaic. Europe began to rebuild new feudal nations among the ruins of the Carolingian Empire, and society demanded more from its leaders than brute, heroic courage. During this period of re-groupment, the *Song of Roland* does not seem to have lost popularity but did gain complexity. We do not know exactly when the story of Roland was combined with the story of Charlemagne to form a single *chanson de geste,* but the effect of introducing a second major hero was to introduce a counterpoint of perspectives into the poem. Roland has the blind, unreflective courage of youth, but Charlemagne has the wisdom (two centuries' worth) of a man whose honor is beyond ques-tion and who has come to value human beings more than heroes. The first half of the *Song of Roland* is Roland's, so Charlemagne's fatigue with the heroic world does not yet dominate the narrative. Neverthe-less, the poet introduces some telling contradictions into his formulaic narrative which belie the oversimplification inherent in his material and suggest that for all its glory, the heroic world is out of joint.

For example, let us consider several passages that deal with the formation of an army of knights and with their preparations to attack the enemy. The first such passage occurs when the pagans prepare to ambush the rearguard of Charlemagne's army as it passes through the mountains:

> Paien s'adubent des osbercs sarazineis,
> Tuit li plusur en sunt dublez en treis.
> Lacent lor elmes mult bons, sarraguzeis,
> Ceignent espees de l'acer vianeis;
> Escuz unt genz, espiez valentineis,
> E gunfanuns blancs e blois e vermeilz.
> Laissent les muls e tuz les palefreiz,
> Es destrers muntent, si chevalchent estreiz,
> Clers fut li jurz e bels fut li soleilz:
> N'unt guarnement que fut ne reflambeit.
> Sunent mil grailles por ço que plus bel seit:
> Granz est la noise, si l'oïrent Franceis. (LXXIX)

> The pagans arm themselves with Saracen mail,
> Almost all their hauberks are triply lined.
> They lace their helmets, Saragossa's best.
> They gird up their swords of Viennese steel.
> They bear fine shields and Valencian lances,
> And banners of white and blue and crimson.
> They leave their palfreys and their mules behind,
> And they ride their battle-horses in close ranks.

> Clear was the day, and beautiful the sun:
> No piece of armor did not flame in the light.
> Great is the noise: a thousand trumpets sound
> Embellishments, and all the Frenchmen hear.

In this passage we get the full chivalric treatment: the splendor of arms, the hordes of soldiers, the glint of weaponry in the sun, and the noise. This is a *topos* common to all epics from Homer to Milton, and a reality of the warrior's world even today. The poet reveals his exultation in lines such as, "They sound a thousand trumpets to make it more beautiful." The jubilant tone of the passage is mirrored in Roland's ecstasy at the prospect of battle: "Ah, may God grant it to us!" (LXXIX). Roland thus provides the traditional hero's response to the opportunity for testing his valor, and he even understands that such occasions for glory will provide excellent material for a future *Song of Roland:* "Let everyone deal out mighty blows, lest bad songs be sung of us!" (LXXIX). We have in effect been shown the epic world through the central hero's eyes.

Soon, however, Oliver acts out of prudence and climbs a hill to assess the pagan forces. Through Oliver's eyes we witness the same formulaic scene all over again, and the same splendors attract emphasis as before—the noise, banners, flaming weapons—but now they are held in the parenthesis, so to speak, of Oliver's less heroic anxiety:

> Oliver es desur un pui muntet.
> Or veit il ben d'Espaigne le regnet
> E Sarrazins, ki tant sunt asemblez.
> Luisent cil elme, ki ad or sunt gemmez,
> E cil escuz e cil osbercs safrez
> E cil espiez, cil gunfanum fermez.
> Sul les escheles ne poet il acunter:
> Tant en i ad que mesure n'en set;
> E lui meïsme en est mult esguaret.
> Cum il einz pout, del pui est avalet,
> Vint as Franceis, tut lur ad acuntet. (LXXXI)

> Oliver climbs to the top of a hill.
> Now he clearly sees the kingdom of Spain,
> And Saracens assembled all in a mass.
> Their helmets shine with gold and studded gems,
> And all those shields and saffron-colored mail,
> And all those swords, and the banners unfurled,

> So many ranks there are, he cannot count.
> He cannot estimate the number of troops.
> Oliver himself is much disturbed.
> Down from the hill he runs as fast as he can,
> And returns to the Frenchmen to tell them all.

Oliver does not tremble with joy at the prospect of battle but runs down the hill as fast as he can—*cum il einz pout*—and tells the Frenchmen all. His behavior is at odds with the heroic timbre of the formulaic description we have just witnessed. As loyal and highly principled as his friend, Oliver is more flexible and brings into the poem an ingredient of pragmatism contrary to the norm of blind heroism that allows Roland not to "see" the pagan army. Oliver is the only person in the *Song of Roland* who sees fit to penetrate beneath the surface of events and to articulate what everyone in his heart already knows—that Ganelon has betrayed the rearguard—and, most important, to propose a course of action that could ward off the disaster.

Once the French are irrevocably committed to mortal combat, however, Roland can permit himself to recognize the truth he earlier had denied. He surveys the on-coming army, and his heroic gladness modulates to solemn self-dedication to a glorious death in combat. Once again, we face the components of the life of chivalric glory, but this time they are seen in the perspective of Roland's own foreknowledge of certain disaster: "Very great will be the emperor's revenge" has the accent of both heroic exultation and acknowledged doom:

> Marsile vient par mi une valee
> Od sa grant ost que il out asemblee.
> .XX. escheles ad li reis anumbrees.
> Luisent cil elme as perres d'or gemmees;
> E cil escuz e cez bronies sasfrees;
> .VII. milie graisles i sunent la menee:
> Grant est la noise par tute la contree.
> Ço dist Rollant: "Oliver, compaign, frere,
> Guenes li fels ad nostre mort juree.
> La traïsun ne poet estre cellee;
> Mult grant venjance en prendrat l'empedere.
> Bataille avrum e forte e aduree,
> Unches mais hom tel ne vit ajustee." (CXII)

> Marsile comes up the middle of the valley
> With his great army that he has assembled.
> The king has gathered twenty corps of battle.
> Their helmet; shine with gold and studded gems,
> And so too the shields, and the saffron mail.
> Seven thousand trumpets sound the charge,
> Great noise resounds throughout the countryside.
> Says Roland: "Oliver, friend and brother,
> The traitor Ganelon has sworn our death.
> His treason can no longer be concealed.
> Very great will be the emperor's revenge.
> A long, hard battle is now close at hand." (CXII)

A final description of an army mustering for attack in the first half of the poem involves Charlemagne and the forward guard. Roland has just sounded his horn, and now Charlemagne and his men understand that their direst misgivings have materialized. They rally quickly to Roland's alarm but already grieve at the fate they know is in store for him. Here if anywhere one might have expected the poet to modulate his description to accord with the tragic circumstances. But not at all—still we see the sun shining on flaming armor, shields painted with flowers, lances, and golden banners:

> Esclargiz est li vespres e li jurz.
> Cuntre le soleil reluisent cil adub,
> Osbercs e helmes i getent grant flabur,
> E cil escuz, ki ben sunt peinz a flurs,
> E cil espiez, cil oret gunfanun. (CXXXVII)

> The day advances into evening.
> The weapons glisten in the light of the sun,
> Hauberks and helmets cast up great flames,
> So too the shields with flowers finely painted;
> So too the swords and the golden banners.

Then, suddenly the tonality of the whole scene is reversed when we see its effect on the emperor. Instead of feeling heroic exaltation at the prospect of battle, Charlemagne (our Roland grown old) experiences only vexation and grief:

> Li empereres cevalchet par irur
> E li Franceis dolenz a curoçus:

> N'i ad celoi ki durement ne plurt,
> E de Rollant sunt en grant poür. (CXXXVII)

> The emperor rides forward in great wrath,
> And the Frenchmen, too, grieving in their anger;
> Every single one was weeping hard,
> And they all fear greatly for Roland's sake.

Clearly, though the poetic language of a less complicated heroic age would tend to dictate the substance of poetic descriptions, our poet succeeds in introducing an expressive counterpoint to the heroic "party line." Indeed, as if to thwart or short-circuit even more the lyricism inherent in the formulaic taking up of arms, the poet evokes another landscape whose dark and sinister valleys and roiled-up waters (themselves perhaps formulaic) visually abuse what we have just seen, making it seem very literally "out of place":

> Halt sunt li pui e tenebrus e grant, AOI.
> Li val parfunt e les ewes curant.
> Sunent cil graisle e derere e devant
> E tuit rachatent encuntre l'olifant.
> Li empereres chevalchet ireement
> E li Franceis curuçus e dolent. . . . (CXXXVIII)

> High are the mountains, shadowy and vast,
> The valleys are deep and the waters swift.
> The trumpets echo behind and ahead,
> And all together answer the Oliphant.
> The emperor is riding forth in wrath,
> And the Frenchmen too, in anger and grief.

By allowing contradictions into his narrative, the poet has questioned his material without rejecting it. He has welcomed the inflexibility of certain traditional motifs and refracted these through a sequence of perspectives, the first of which is Roland's and the last Charlemagne's: Roland is foolish and proud, the emperor old and wise. The emperor has come to value men more than heroes. His tragedy, his isolation (symbolized by two hundred years of age), is that he can in no way—not even in language—change the heroic formulas of a society that has become alien to him.

Nevertheless, Roland is decidedly the hero of the first half of this epic, and the poet remains committed to the virtuosity of his own formulaic material. Our suspicions that the poet may see more widely than his hero must remain dormant as the first half of the poem draws to a climactic close. Feeling the approach of death after he has been mortally wounded in his solitary struggle with the pagan masses, Roland staggers to a hilltop, where he tries to break his sword Durendal. Durendal symbolizes all of Roland's past conquests; indeed, as we shall see later, it even personifies his indomitable, heroic self-hood. The sword will not break but springs back up toward the sky, and one last, brief time we see a weapon gleaming in the sun. Because the audience has been well indoctrinated in the formulaic trappings of the warrior's world, this single detail suffices now to evoke the *Gestalt* of a whole glorious ethic. Now, Roland's condition is that of a solitary dying man who looks back on a life of hardship and suffering for Christ and Charlemagne. His joy at seeing the flash of sunlight on steel reveals that he remains steadfast, even in the sting of death, to those ideals of chivalric heroism by which he has lived:

> Roland strikes his sword on the onyx stone.
> The steel grinds, but does not break or chip.
> And when he sees that it will never break,
> Roland laments to himself for his sword:
> "Ah, Durendal! So fine and clear and bright!
> How you shine and flame out in the sunlight!
> Charles was in the valley of Maurienne
> When, through his angel, God commanded him
> To let you gird one of his ranking counts:
> Thus, the noble emperor armed me with you.
> I conquered both Anjou and Brittany,
> And then I conquered both Poitou and Maine. . . ." (CVXXII)

One danger of the formulaic theory is that it can explain too much and make us blind to other equally important considerations about language in the poem. Certainly, if Charlemagne allows himself to be drawn into a tragic web of personalities beneath him, it is not only because the language of his world is committed to inflexible formulas of heroic art. Charlemagne's impassivity reflects deeper attitudes about the very nature of language as a social instrument. Like Homer's *Iliad*, the *Song of Roland* grows out of an epic tradition whose heroes characteristically live a life of action, not one of words. In the *Song of Roland* discourse itself is seen as a form of action. This is not true of the *Odyssey*, which is also a formulaic poem, whose hero talks himself through the world more than he fights in it. When one reads such scenes as Roland's defiance of Ganelon or Ganelon's stormy visit to Marsile's court, one is inevitably struck by the interpenetration of language and gesture: in the first scene, Ganelon leaps up and throws off his cape when Roland names him for the embassy; Roland laughs out his sarcasm; Ganelon drops Charlemagne's glove. In the second scene, Marsile trembles with rage at Ganelon's message and brandishes a spear at him; Ganelon draws his sword "the length of two fingers" from its sheath; Ganelon throws off his cape; Marsile lunges to attack him; Ganelon backs off to retreat; Ganelon and Marsile come to terms and later kiss each other on the face and chin. Discourse in the *Song of Roland* is not a sphere in its own right and does not stand apart from the fabric of violence as a verbal realm opposed to action. It is not impossible to find analogous situations in our day where the word has approximately the same relationship to the deed. For example, on the football field, discourse serves to communicate the strategy of a forthcoming play, to exert the player to "beat" (if not "kill") his opponent, and to convey the concerted emotions of spectators who vicariously participate in the violence before their eyes. It would be unthinkable for two football captains to sit down and talk things out instead of "having" them out in a game.

For the poet of the *Song of Roland*, as for the poet of the *Iliad*, discourse remains deeply rooted in that physical world in which his figures move. Discourse begins and ends in action, for ontologically they are at the same level. Thus, the five council scenes in the poem do not replace or even redirect action, but are part of it. The heroic ethos of the *Roland* is remarkably close to that of the *Iliad*, and especially of Achilles, who says to crafty Odysseus:

> ". . . I detest as the doorways of Death, I detest that man
> Who hides one thing in the depth of his heart and speaks forth another.
> But I will speak to you the way it seems best to me. . . ." [6]

If an exception to this attitude exists in the *Song of Roland*, we may find it in Ganelon, who is a master of words and a devil. Ganelon first talks the French barons into rejecting Roland's strategy for dealing with the Saracens; he skillfully deceives Blancandrin into believing that Roland alone is to blame for the war against the pagans; he artfully exposes his plan for treason while they travel to Marsile's court; he convinces Marsile to play along with his deceit; finally, when

Roland blows his horn, Ganelon lies openly to his emperor: "There is no battle! You are old and white as a flower, and such words make you seem childish" (CXXXIV).

Even Oliver, whose role is one of restraint and discretion, believes that a knight must not give himself over to vain discourse: when language becomes divorced from what lies immediately at hand, one's duty is to lay it aside and take up the sword. Thus when Oliver perceives that Roland is resolved not to sound his horn and that the fighting has already begun, he formally renounces discourse ("I do not want to speak") in favor of the cry "Munjoie!"—this is the cry of action *par excellence:* "Whoever heard them cry 'Munjoie!' would never forget such noble vassalage" (XCII).

Ganelon, then, is the only figure in the *Song of Roland* in whom the slightest discrepancy between word and deed, between appearance and reality, is ever present. Adam Parry says of the *Iliad*:

> Since the economy of the formulaic style confines speech to accepted patterns which all men assume to be true, there need never be a fundamental distinction between speech and reality; and between thought and reality—for thought and speech are not distinguished; or between appearance and reality—for the language of society is the way society makes things seem.[7]

We should not be surprised that Ganelon, who has betrayed the norms of his society, should use language differently from other men in the poem. We must remember that ideally, the cement of feudal society was an oath of faith between man and man, and when language became detached from a commitment of faith—faith of any kind—it became a tool of subversion. Achilles and Charlemagne are the most powerful men in the world, yet Achilles cannot bring himself to leave the Achaeans who have cheated him and sail away to a new world; it does not occur to Charlemagne to lift a finger against the tragedy that weaves itself about him. In both cases, there is a failure of language as a tool to analyze the world and to proffer an alternative to the horror of a present reality. Like Achilles, Charlemagne is cognitively circumscribed by the unreflective quality of his language—and this is the language of the poem—and is helplessly caught in an earthly community that is destined to destroy its better self. As if the poet wished to insist upon the deadly potency of the spoken word, he causes Ganelon's lie to Charlemagne (that the Saracen troops have been swallowed up by the sea) to become a terrifying prophecy of truth: Charlemagne will indeed drive the pagans *en masse* into the river Ebro (CLXXX). Let this be a lesson to medieval liars!

The close alliance between word and deed in the *Song of Roland* imparts great strength and virility to its poetry. As we shall have occasion to note in another chapter, most of the formulas in the *Song of Roland* fulfill not only the exigencies of the *ear* (and the meter) but also the exigencies of the *eye* as the poet draws us into a world of things and movement. Word counts run the risk of being as subjective as value judgments; nevertheless one senses that the whole density and kinesis of the narrative in the *Song of Roland* derives, more than in most poetry, from an especially heavy reliance on substantives and verbs. The formulas, too, it must be remembered, have no absolute metrical length, but can be shortened, extended, or broken up and scattered through a whole line or two. A formula is as much a unit of space, mass, or action as it is a metrical unit of sound. The following two highly formulaic *laisses* will illustrate that concreteness that provides the fullest basis for knowledge in the heroic mentality, and even for communication as well:

> Count Roland rides onto the battlefield,
> With Durendal, which hacks and slices well.
> He spreads great harm among the Saracens.
> What a sight: man after man he kills;
> Bright blood is everywhere upon the ground!
> His hauberk and his arms are red with blood,
> His horse, too, about the neck and shoulders.
> Oliver, as well, is no less quick to strike,
> And the twelve peers, who all fight blamelessly.
> The Frenchmen strike, then multiply their blows.
> Some of the pagans die, while others faint.
> The archbishop says, "Blessed be our barons!"
> "Munjoie!" he cries, which is the call of Charles. (CV)

> Oliver now rides right into the mob.
> His spear is broken, only a piece remains.
> He goes to strike a pagan named Malun.
> He breaks his shield, ornate with gold and flowers.
> He knocks both of his eyes out of his head.
> His brain spills and runs down to his feet.

Down he falls, with seven hundred dead men.
He kills then Turgis, and then Esturguz.
His spear breaks and splinters at the handle.
Thus speaks Roland: "Friend, what are you doing?
What good is a club in such a battle?
Steel and Iron are what should be used here.
Where is your sword, which is called 'Halteclere'!?
The handguard is gold, the pummel crystal."
"I could not draw it! too much work to do!" (CVI)

Admirably suited to experience that is concrete, language in the
Song of Roland is correspondingly weak when dealing with abstractions, generalities, and the area of subjectivity. The poet always eval-
uates his characters in terms of a specific role rather than in the light
of any final, abstract ethical generality. One is not usually "good" in
the *Song of Roland*—one is a "good *vassal*" or a "good *baron*"; or
else one strikes "good *blows*" or carries a "good *sword*." In such cases
the word "good" does not derive its meaning from any ultimate
notion of good and evil, but rather from some immediate, physical
attribute.[8] Often men will be described adjectively as *vassal, baron,*
which means that they are good, or as *serf,* which means that they
are evil. In other words, ethical judgments are made on the basis of
extrinsic situations, not of intrinsic qualities. Even Charlemagne, the
emperor, is *vassal.* As Roland says, "The French are good: they will
strike like vassals." In this poem it is impossible to know a man
apart from his acts.

Occasionally, however, we see the poet groping for abstractions. The
word bon*tet* (good*ness*) appears twice in the poem, once in the words
of Ganelon as he praises his emperor's "goodness" before Marsile
(XL), and once again in the poet's description of the "goodness" of
Charlemagne's sword, Joyeuse (CLXXXIII). In the first case, however, the context suggests that *bontet* means prowess or valor of a
physical kind; in the second, the *bontet* of Charlemagne's sword derives from a relic of Christ's passion mounted in the handle. When
the poet tries to tell us that Roland never liked any evil man, he falls
back on a curious redundancy: *ne malvais hume de male part* (CLIX)
is confusing until we understand that the poet instinctively reinforces
his abstract ethical judgment (a "*bad* man") by rooting it in a more
concrete spatial axis ("from a bad *part*"). To shift the accent of

Horace's phrase, we may say that from the beginning to the end of the *Song of Roland* we are constantly not "in the *midst* of things" but "in the midst of *things*."

Even though the poet shows signs of unrest within the traditional framework of ethical values he has inherited, he nevertheless remains in it; hence, a lord is good; a vassal is good; a serf is bad. However, beyond the feudal hierarchy of values in the poem is a larger and self-evident moral distinction: Christians are good and Saracens are evil. The Saracens are feudal like the Christians, yet the poet and his audience are so ideologically sure of themselves that the former can lavish feudal terms of praise on the Saracens to magnify their evil and not be misunderstood.

Thus, the poet can say of Blancandrin, Ganelon's pagan colleague in conspiracy, "In vassalage he was very much a knight; he showed courage in helping his lord" (III). These formulas of excellence are the means by which the Saracens' capacity for evil is exaggerated. In the same way, Milton can describe Satan sitting "exalted" on his throne in Hell, "by merit raised / to that bad eminence . . ." (*Paradise Lost,* II.5). Or, again, the medieval poet praises the thieving pagan who attempts to steal Roland's sword as he is dying. The poet tells us that the Arab has soiled his body by smearing it with blood and that he has passed himself off as a dead man on the battlefield—this is a grotesque, but common, ploy of cowardice. Then he adds, "he was beautiful and strong and of great vassalage" (CLIX). Such an obvious contradiction may be understood in the same way as is one's saying to us that his sprained ankle is "good and sore." The Saracens are "good and bad."

Ethically, the *Song of Roland* tends to deal with effects and not causes. More exactly, we should say that in this poem it is impossible to distinguish between them. In other words, the language of the *Song of Roland* is well equipped to represent the social and political side of the feudal world, but it does not test the spiritual motives behind them. One could apply to this poem a descriptive anthropological term, which has also been applied to the *Iliad*: the *Song of Roland* expresses a *shame* culture instead of a *guilt* culture. I say this because the fear of God, despite the Christian context of the poem, is not the strongest moral force its characters know; rather, it is respect for public opinion. The enjoyment of *honour* is more their goal than a quiet conscience.

One reason why the poet does not explore the spiritual dimension of his characters is that he lived in a culture that was linguistically compartmented and stratified, where the diverse functions of language (religious, judicial, communicative, artistic, etc.) were fulfilled in diverse and well-differentiated spheres of language and style.[9] A stratification of styles and even of language-functions is not easily understood in a linguistic community such as our own, where there has been an unprecedented stylistic leveling and where everybody from the President to the policeman is taught to talk from the hip. The *Song of Roland,* however, originated in and was destined for an exclusive audience, one of extraordinary ethical solidarity, whose members automatically understood the moral system operating in the language and idiom of the poem. One critic has suggested that this explains why the poem is so paratactic, that is, why it can set forth its propositions without those conjunctions, adverbs, and prepositions that normally would link phrase to phrase in an intelligible sequence where causality is clear.[10] The culture shared by the poet's audience could be counted on to provide intellectual continuity. My own feeling is that the vernacular French oral tradition was simply unconcerned with the subtleties of reasoned, reflective narrative such as we find in the cultural tradition of medieval Latin. The French is a vernacular language of action; by contrast, the language of the medieval Latin epic, its cultural bedfellow, tends to be didactic and intellectual. A Latin epic such as Eupolemius' *Messiad* has for its narrative substance, allegory; for its heroes, Biblical figures or personifications of virtues and vices; and for its action, sermonizing harangues.[11] The two kinds of poem play complementary roles in medieval culture, each stressing a different area of experience. The latter, destined to preoccupy the "busy leisure" (*negotiosissimum otium*) of the contemplative man in the cloister, who believed that there was no exterior path to the knowledge of God, asks its reader to look beyond the letter of the tale and to contemplate the eternal, spiritual truths it contains; the former is destined for men of active life who (without necessarily being less pious) accept passionate and physical daring as the best indication of moral worth.[12] The poet says of the duel between Baligant and Charlemagne: "This battle can never end, until one of them recognizes his wrong" (CCLIX). So too, Baligant learns of his moral error only when the tide of events turns against him:

> Baligant sees that his banner is fallen
> And then he sees Mohammed's flag is down:
> The Emir now begins to understand
> That he is wrong and Charlemagne is right. (CCLVII)

In a poem where discourse is a form of action, action is likewise a form of discourse. By virtue of his *gestes,* Roland is in a sense the "author" of the *Song of Roland.* Like Achilles, he knows that if his actions are worthy, men will sing a "good" song and not a "bad" one about him. The poet, for his part, gives himself over anonymously to his narrative, for the excellence of the material guarantees that the song will be good. Yet if the poet effaces himself one minute to allow the poem to "write itself," the next minute he comes alive as an oral performer and lives out the passions of his hero, making them his own. In the heat of the oral performance, Roland's excellence becomes the poet's; the hero becomes an artist, and the artist becomes a hero, transformed by his own song.

❧ IV ❧

NARRATIVE SETTING AND THE
LAISSE SIMILAIRE

The *Song of Roland* falls roughly into four principal parts: the dispute between Ganelon and Roland, the battle leading to the death of Roland, Charlemagne's revenge on the pagans, and Ganelon's trial and punishment. Readers are unanimous in their feeling that the second part of the *Song of Roland* is the most powerful. In this chapter I shall explore two intimately related aspects of the poet's narrative technique which contribute to that power: first, his use of settings in the physical world to approach, define, and amplify the emotionality of his characters; and second, his adaptation of the *laisse* form to sharpen the dramatic outlines of his heroes and their deeds.[1] In the following chapter we may then devote our whole attention to Roland himself.

Let us first examine in some detail the *laisses* that begin the account of the disaster at Ronceval. Formulaic though they are, they bear close attention, not only because they evoke a setting that is full of human implications and anticipates the tragedy shortly to follow, but also because they exemplify the peculiar subtlety of effect which this poetic style at its best can attain. I cite the first *laisse:*

> High are the mountains, shadowy the valleys;
> The rocks are greyish brown, the gorges strange.
> On that day the French passed by in great pain.
> Full fifteen leagues could their march be heard.
> When they came to the land of their lineage,
> They looked over Gascony, their lords' land;
> Then they remembered the fiefs that they held,
> The maidens at home, and their noble wives.
> Not a one did not weep from tenderness.
> Charlemagne is most anguished of them all:
> On Spain's border he has left his nephew.
> Pity takes him; he weeps; he cannot hold back. (LXVI)

These twelve lines constitute a true narrative unity, having its own internal structure and coherence (I shall return to this point later). The first line sketches the physical setting in which a great human tragedy is about to unfold: "High are the mountains, shadowy the valleys." The polarities of this setting—mountain and valley, sunny height and dark lowland (as in "I shall walk through the valley of the shadow of death")—will be inextricably involved in the polarities of experience that the central heroes are fated to undergo, and this verse will be repeated as a motif with variations many times during the second part of the poem. The poet situates the audience's eye somewhere between these extremes, and this mid-point is expressed chromatically in the grey-brown of the rock. The poet has created a backdrop which perfectly accommodates the precarious emotional balance in the minds of the French as they negotiate the Pyrenees. Like a Greek chorus grieving in advance for the house of Agamemnon, the French knights weep because they know full well (as the audience knows) that a catastrophe is at hand, one of human temperaments that are heroic and exalted and yet destined to fall. Now the spaces of this setting are quickened by the noise of the soldiers' footsteps resounding as they pass through the fearsome gorges in "great pain." By situating the soldiers midway between Spain (the land of suffering and death) and France (the land of security and love, of lords, maidens, and wives whom they long to see again) the poet reinforces the polarities of height and depth and light and dark and fashions around his figures a spatial field which mirrors the complexities of their state of mind: "Not a one did not weep for tenderness." Having completed this landscape of heroic emotion, the poet closes his *laisse* by centering on Charlemagne, unique in power and supreme in anguish, upon whose shoulders the ultimate burden of the tragedy must fall.

What follows in the text renders the contents of the preceding *laisse* more intelligible and explicit—frequently in the *Song of Roland* one *laisse* will contain the seed of the next:

> The twelve peers remain behind in Spain.
> Twenty thousand Frenchmen are with them.
> None feels fear and none is afraid to die.
> The emperor is on his way to France.
> He keeps his face concealed beneath his cape.
> The Duke of Naimes rides close beside the king,
> And says to him, "What weighs upon you so?"

Charles replies: "Whoever asks offends me!
My grief is great; I cannot hold it back.
France will be destroyed by Ganelon.
Last night an angel's vision came to me
That Ganelon broke my lance between my hands:
Thus, my nephew in the rear is doomed,
For I have left him in a hostile land.
O God! should I lose him, none can take his place." (LXVII)

Charlemagne's gesture of hiding his face beneath his cape is stark and powerful. Intensity of passion frequently imposes a kind of emblematic mannerism on the characters of this poem, in defiance, of course, of the norms of reality by which ordinary men act. The result of such distortion is an extreme purity of expression, which recalls the extravagantly stylized gestures of romanesque sculpture such as at Vézelay or Autun. Perhaps one could say of all romanesque art what one may say about the *Song of Roland,* that movements of heroic passion have absolute priority over the normal perspectives of space or time which relate an object or person to a coherent *context.* As is the case with poetry of our own day, verisimilitude (or what we now often call "realism") has little value in the *Song of Roland.*

Stunned though he may be by the directness of gesture in this poem, the reader is likely to feel some perplexity because he cannot penetrate this exterior setting with any certainty of discovering the underlying motives. Why, we may wonder, does Charlemagne labor so hard to conceal his grief from his fellow soldiers? Why is Charlemagne so reluctant to interpret his dream of the previous night, which prophesies Ganelon's treason? Why does Charlemagne resist foreknowledge? Surely Charlemagne does not hide his despair in order to sustain the morale of his men, as Aeneas does, for example, while he is at sea in Book I of the *Aeneid.* I believe, rather, that Charlemagne is motivated by a peculiarly medieval regard for the potency of the spoken word: he understands that once the prophecy of the forthcoming tragedy has been verbalized, the tragedy is one step closer to happening. In this poem the word is as irrevocable as the deed.

The third *laisse* (LXVIII) summarizes in general terms what has preceded in the two previous *laisses.* Charlemagne weeps, and a hundred thousand Frenchmen grieve with him. The French knights have a choral function here. By their multitude, they amplify the emotions that Charlemagne himself has felt; and because they too are spectators to the action of this poem, they guide and intensify the reactions of the audience.

It could be argued that the mountain setting in the *Song of Roland* was dictated by a historical memory of Ronceval, the setting of the disaster, which is indeed surrounded by the Pyrenees. But when we notice that the poet situates Saragossa in the mountains as well, we realize that geography concerns this poet primarily for its metaphorical expressiveness. For example, just before the battle between the Christians and pagans, Oliver climbs to the top of a hill because he suspects that trouble is at hand. The poet tells us three times in a row that he has climbed the hill, emphasizing through repetition the significance of Oliver's act. He sees the plain below swarming with enemy troops and knows at once that Ganelon has betrayed the rearguard. Here the external world is again made to dramatize a moral state of mind. Roland, by contrast, has remained in the valley because he does not care to recognize what is obvious; thus, when Oliver accuses Ganelon of treason, Roland silences him with anger. He is spoiling for battle and wants his men to forget about Ganelon so that they will direct their hostility toward the Saracens instead. Through physical positions—Oliver up on a hill giving wise advice and Roland below, arrogantly resisting the counsel of his best friend—the poet reinforces the spiritual relationship between the two knights in a way made explicit by the next *laisse:* "Roland is bold and Oliver is wise." Later, however, when Roland is mortally wounded, it will be *his* turn to climb the hill (CLXVIII) that marks moral pre-eminence.

The exchange that takes place between Roland and Oliver while the army bears down upon the rearguard is nearly one hundred lines long. The poet has momentarily arrested his narrative in order to emphasize the qualities that make these men what they are. The central part of the dispute occupies three *laisses,* starting with LXXXIII. Such sequences, usually involving three *laisses,* appear frequently in the Oxford version of the poem and are called *laisses similaires:*

> Oliver says, "The pagans have great strength;
> The Frenchmen seem to me so very few.
> Roland, my companion, sound your horn.
> Charles will hear it; the army will return."
> Roland answers, "This would be great madness!
> I would lose my honor in sweet France.
> Now I must strike great blows with Durendal

And bloody my blade to its hilt of gold.
Woe to the treacherous pagans in this pass!
I swear that all of them are doomed to die." (LXXXIII)

"Roland, my companion, sound your horn.
Charles will hear and make his men return.
The king will save us with his baronage."
Roland answers, "May it not please God
That kin of mine be blamed because of me,
Or that France should ever be disgraced!
Thus I shall strike out hard with Durendal,
My good sword, with which I gird my side.
You shall see the blade completely bloodied.
Woe to the pagans that have gathered here:
I swear to you that all are doomed to die." (LXXXIV)

"Roland, my companion, sound your Oliphant,
So Charles will hear it, who is in the pass.
I swear to you, the French will soon return."
"May it not please God!" is Roland's answer.
"May it not be said by any man alive
That I blew my horn because of pagans.
My kinsmen shan't be blamed because of me.
As soon as I am in this mighty war,
I'll strike one thousand seven hundred blows.
You'll see Durendal's steel become all bloody.
The French are good, and they will strike like vassals.
For those of Spain there will be no escape." (LXXXV)

The three *laisses* here contain ten, eleven, and twelve lines respectively, and each has roughly the same structure: first an exasperated plea by Oliver for Roland to sound his horn; then Roland's refusal. Roland answers Oliver each time with a different explanation of his decision to stand and fight: personal honor, family honor, and finally, the defense of Christianity itself. These three answers are obviously meant to show how a traditional, aristocratic temperament responds to challenge by an enemy. One will notice, however, a curious lack of logical development in the argument. This is an exchange of high words, as the poet says (LXXXVII), but not of ideas. The *laisse similaire* fixes each man in his respective viewpoint, and no progression or synthesis of ideas is posible. There is only reiteration, as if Roland's answers were three aspects of what was in reality a single, instantaneous reaction. At any rate, by the end of the third *laisse,* Roland's inflexibility is all too apparent. When confronted a fourth time by Oliver's conviction that discretion is the better part of valor, Roland answers right from the heart of the heroic code:

> "May it not please God or please his angels
> That France should lose her honor because of me.
> I would rather die than suffer shame.
> The more we strike, the more the emperor loves us." (LXXXXVI)

Twice more Roland voices his determination to resist the Saracen attack, and in *laisse* LXXXVIII we arrive at the ideological core of his heroic outlook:

> "The emperor, who left us with these Frenchmen,
> Selected twenty thousand of the best.
> He knew that not a one was cowardly.
> For his lord a man must suffer great pain;
> He must endure great cold and mighty heat;
> A man must sacrifice both flesh and blood.
> Strike with your lance, and I with Durendal,
> My good sword, that the king himself gave me.
> If I should die, the man who gains my sword
> Will say, 'This was a noble vassal's sword!' " (LXXXVIII)

To this, in the chivalric code, there is no answer, and Oliver gives up pleading. With *laisse* LXXXIX the poem recovers its narrative tempo.

In such passages as these, the *laisse* tends away from straight narrative toward a strophic form with recapitulations. Generally, these passages occur at crucial points in the story, such as when Charlemagne asks his barons to appoint an ambassador to Marsile's court or when Roland decides (later) to sound his horn or when Charlemagne grieves for his fallen nephew. Basically, the more the *laisse similaire* becomes strophic, the more the content of the passage becomes lyrical. Lyrical poetry is not usually narrative in content but characteristically exalts moments of great psychological significance (despair, anxiety, revelations, etc.). The movement of the *Song of Roland* is continuously subject to a tension of two contradictory forces: the forward thrust of narrative and the restraining power of lyric. At any moment in the poem one tendency or the other will prevail. If we imagine the narrative line propelled by action as a vertical axis, we may imagine the moments of retard as interruptions or dilations, which comprise a horizontal axis:

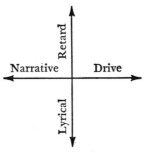

These two axes correspond partially, of course, to the poem's dual nature as both song and story.

The *laisse similaire* may also be considered as an outgrowth of the manner in which the poet actually perceives the gestures of his heroes. We noticed earlier that he feels a need to situate heroic action in an appropriate spatial setting, and the *laisse* form readily offers a rhetorical equivalent; each *laisse* can be built around a single gesture or episode, such as an outburst of emotion or a blow struck in combat. The function of the *laisse* is so intimately related to the function of the spatial setting that when there is a series of such gestures, the poet will frequently reiterate the setting as he begins the next *laisse*. Here, for example, is the ending of *laisse* XI, where Charlemagne's preparations for the council of barons are described:

> Next, the king went out beneath a pine tree,
> And summoned his barons out to council:
> He wants the best of France to give their guidance. (XI)

Laisse XII could just as easily have begun with a list of these barons, except that the poet felt a necessity to repeat the context first:

> The emperor goes out beneath a pine tree,
> And summons his barons out to council,
> Duke Ogier, and Archbishop Turpin. . . . (XII)

On some occasions the poet's recapitulation of a setting in the new *laisse* is designed to intensify a specific emotional effect. Thus, we read in *laisse* CCLXVII how Charlemagne returns to France to try Ganelon for treason:

> Charles rides home through the valleys and mountains.
> He wants no delay before he reaches Aix.
> He rides and rides until he reaches his steps.
> Once arrived at his sovereign palace,
> He summons his judges by messenger,
> Bavarians, Saxons, Lorrainians,
> Frisians, Germans, Burgundians, Potevines,
> Normans and Britons, the wisest in France.
> And then the trial of Ganelon begins. (CCLXVII)

Charlemagne faces also, however, the sad duty of confronting Aude, who is both Oliver's sister and Roland's fiancée, with the news of the disaster at Ronceval. A simple conjunction or adverb could have linked the narration of this task to the preceding act of summoning the barons; instead, the poet repeats himself in order to grant the fullest possible impact to the scene of Aude's discovery. The repetition here is less textual than it is dramatic:

> The emperor has come back from Spain.
> He comes back to Aix, the capital of France.
> He enters the palace and goes to his room.
> To him comes Aude, a beautiful maiden.
> She speaks thus: "Where is my captain, Roland,
> Who has promised to take me as his wife?"
> Charlemagne suffers in anguish and pain.
> He weeps from his eyes and pulls his white beard:
> "Child, sweet friend, you ask for a man who is dead!" (CCLXVII)

In the latter *laisse* the poet recapitulates Charlemagne's return but omits the idea of his impatience to restore political order. The whole of the second description is redesigned to bring out emotions appropriate to the encounter with Aude, who falls dead at the news. Once again we observe the poet's tendency to frame human emotions in an appropriate dramatic setting, which easily overrides any concern for chronological coherence in his narrative.

Perhaps the most distinctive quality of the *laisse* as a narrative form is its flexibility. The average number of lines in a *laisse* in this poem is fourteen, but the longest has thirty-five (CCXXVII) and the shortest five (XXVI, LX). Because deeds are the real substance of the *Song of Roland*, the glory of the *laisse* is its pliability in serving the virtuosity of heroic action. The contours of the *laisse* ebb and flow with the waves of action in the poem, so that the tale seems to be creating its own form. The poet never attempts to draw the reader into the sphere of his own artistic consciousness, as Virgil does, for example, but subordinates his medium at every moment to the task of recounting an inherited tale. One result of these procedures is that we feel far closer to Roland, Oliver, and Turpin as they fulfill themselves in violent deeds than to the nameless narrator. Another and more troubling result is that the only continuity in the poem lies in the actions themselves. The *laisse* form does not situate heroic deeds in a logical, linear, or even temporal sequence; on the contrary, it breaks up the sequence of events into distinct and autonomous blocks of movement and space, each with its specific center of interest.[2] This irreducible, brick-like structure of action makes the poem seem unintelligible on any other terms. Whereas later *chansons de geste* will tend toward amplification and self-interpretation, this poem at its best sustains uninterrupted awe by its stark succession of *laisses*. Ideas have low priority in the *Roland,* and the reader must shift for himself if he wishes to formulate what thematic connections bind *laisse* to *laisse* and episode to episode.[3] Superficially, the parataxis of style and action in the *Roland* makes the poem seem strangely modern (and even cinematic) to some, and it is true that most poetry of our own age has also rejected coherence at the surface of thought and image, thereby challenging the reader to unleash the powers of his own imagination. In both kinds of poetry, to understand is to participate in a higher and purer order of existence. The modern poet draws us away from the ordinary world into the dissociated poetic imagination in whose salutary sphere action is the gesture of an aesthetic sensibility. The medieval poet, by contrast, for whom the notion of art for art's sake would have been incomprehensible, draws us into a realm that is apart from the ordinary world only because its heroes are grander and more violent than we. These heroes still affirm by their struggles, however, the value of a life *in medias res,* of action in a world where glory and high deeds are felt to be not only possible but necessary for anyone who aspires (as Roland does) to a hero's welcome in Paradise.

❧ V ❧

THE PASSION AND DEATH

OF ROLAND

If we study the progress of the battle between the French rearguard and the pagans at Ronceval, we will notice that the poet maintains a deliberate pace in the unfolding of his tale. The battle is described in eighty-four *laisses:* the first blow is struck in *laisse* XCIII, and Roland dies in *laisse* CLXXVII. With a characteristic rhythm of alternation, the poet intersperses the battle narrative with focal points in the personal experience of his heroes, which allow us to trace the progress of their self-fulfillment in impassioned, monumental deeds. Every ten *laisses,* roughly, lead to some new phase in the destinies of Roland and his companions as they undergo the consequences of their fatal choice to fight alone against the pagan hordes. Some of these moments are lyrical highpoints in the poem.

Roland strikes the first blow of the war in *laisse* XCIII—primacy in epic is always a sign of pre-eminence. Exultantly confident that the pagans will be slaughtered and their treasure his by evening, Roland boasts like a Homeric warrior as he cuts Marsile's nephew (his own Saracen counterpart) in two with his sword:

> "Charles was gallant to leave us in the hills.
> Sweet France won't lose her glory on this day.
> Strike out, you Frenchmen! Ours is the first blow.
> We are in the right, these wretches wrong!" (XCIII)

During the nine *laisses* that follow, Oliver and eight other French barons follow Roland's defiant example, and each individually tastes the joys of splitting bejewelled helmets (and their contents) with Christian steel. At the tenth *laisse* (CIII), the pagans rally to the horn of Margariz; and in the following *laisse,* Roland again becomes the center of attention as he draws his sword Durendal and with a second "epic" blow cuts both Chernuble and his horse in half. Death is everywhere, but it is without gravity, without pain, and seems almost to be a part of life itself. The poet echoes the mood of his heroes ("The battle is marvelous and vast!"), and Roland seconds the poet by delivering a further thrust of his sword with the all-insulting boast:

> "Serf! You'll rue this day!
> Mohammed will not give you any aid.
> Fools like you will never win a battle." (CIV)

Through the nine *laisses* that follow, the poet portrays the exuberance of the French as they witness each other's triumphs. One would think that the warrior's world was the happiest of places:

> Lord Oliver has drawn his mighty sword,
> As Roland, his companion, long had urged.
> He brandishes his sword as a knight should,
> And strikes a pagan, Justin de Val Feree.
> He splits the head in two right down the middle,
> He cleaves the body and the saffron mail,
> And the fine saddle with gold and studded gems,
> And cleaves the horse's back right through the spine:
> He slaughters both before him on the field.
> This speaks Roland: "Now I know you, brother!
> Charles, the emperor, loves us for such blows!"
> From all sides the cry "Munjoie!" resounds. (CVII)'

The poet remains aware, however, as his characters do not, of the tenuousness of the heroic warrior's joy; for just when glory seems certain, the tide of events turns and the Saracens gain the upper hand. Joy gives way to apocalyptic horror as the skies darken with a miraculous eclipse and supernatural storms ravage the whole of "sweet France":

> In France a miraculous storm breaks out,
> A tempest bringing thunder and great wind,
> Rain and hailstones beyond all measure;
> Lightning strikes both suddenly and often,
> And violent earthquakes ravage all the land. (CX)

Reflecting the general eschatological concern of the eleventh century, Charlemagne's men all believe that the end of the world is at hand. They do not know that the calamity is a prefiguration of Roland's martyrdom, which is already imminent. Marsile approaches him now with a massive army, and Roland admits (for the first time) that

Ganelon has organized a fatal conspiracy against him and the French rearguard. This moment marks an important transition, for Roland's mood now modulates from exultation to grim determination as he resolves to fulfill his commitment to the heroic code, a code whose premises are the very foundation of the traditional *chanson de geste:*

> "A long and painful war is now before us.
> Never before have men seen such a clash.
> I will strike with Durendal, my sword,
> And you, companion, will strike with Halteclere.
> In so many places have we carried them!
> So many battles have they won for us!
> Bad songs must never be sung of our swords." (CXII)

For another six *laisses* the battle grows more intense, and during this time the French begin to suffer heavier and heavier losses as their best knights throw themselves on the enemy, inspired by the archbishop's guarantee of automatic salvation. The first of the twelve peers to die is Engeler de Gascogne, in *laisse* CXVI; Sansun, in *laisse* CXVIII; Anseis, in *laisse* CXX; Gerin, Gerier, Berenger, and two other French knights, in *laisse* CXXII. Roland now perceives that his companions are beginning to despair. As a good leader must, he sets an example of defiance in *laisses* CXXIV–CXXV, where he flattens the pagan Grandonie in the best formulaic style and succeeds in reviving his men's courage. Finally the pagans are put to rout in *laisse* CXXVI.

The remission is brief, though, and during the nine *laisses* that follow, the French lose all but sixty men. Aware that there is no escape, Roland decides that the moment has come when he may sound his horn, Oliphant, with impunity and summon help from Charlemagne. But this decision leads to a second quarrel with his friend Oliver. It begins when Roland looks about him and sees that his companions are being slaughtered:

> "So many vassals struck down dead!
> Now we must grieve for beautiful France,
> Stripped and empty from the loss of such barons!
> Ah, King, Friend! Why are you not here with us?
> Oliver, my brother, what are we to do?" (CXXVIII)

Though the situation is obviously the consequence of his earlier decision to reject aid and to prove his honor as a knight, he is not conscious of any error on his part. His question is simply that of a leader who seeks advice (*consilium*). But Oliver answers haughtily that he has no advice; indeed, he would rather lose his life than be shamed by such a call for help. Here, Roland and Oliver plainly have been made to change roles: Roland is at last wise and Oliver is at last bold. Understanding that rescue is impossible and that his status as a hero is now beyond question, Roland can summon Charlemagne without compromising himself; the decision, now, would be strategic and not moral. Oliver, on the other hand, for all his wisdom, is as devoted to heroic honor as Roland and believes that this code does not permit any second thoughts once a commitment has been made. Both, in a sense, are again right, and I believe that the inversion of roles is an attempt on the poet's part to ennoble his characters by allowing each to share the virtue of the other. Yet each, again, guards a principle that is finally irreconcilable with the other. When the two principles collide, as in this quarrel, paralysis in the heroic world is the only possible result. If the heroic world is to endure at all, bold-ness must always carry off the victory from wisdom—as the earlier confrontation between Roland and Charlemagne abundantly shows. In the quarrel between Roland and Oliver, the poet points again to the weakness of the system whose glories he celebrates.

As was the case in their first quarrel, Roland does not discernibly react to the substance of Oliver's criticism; and instead of thesis, an-tithesis, and synthesis, there is a simple reiteration of inflexible po-sitions. Our poet is unprepared to operate in an intellectual system, and he seems to perceive the argument here as an exalted conflict of personalities, or as a struggle of opposing impulses in the same per-sonality, rather than as a logical problem with complex moral ramifica-tions.[1] Discourse in the *Song of Roland* is never capable of speculation beyond what is rooted in the physical world immediately at hand. Thus, Archbishop Turpin, the peace-making warrior of Christ, scuttles the argument before it gets very far, and does so without compromis-ing either party: "To sound the horn would not save us; yet to sound it would be better. The king would come and avenge us" (CXXXII).

An impressive feature of the quarrel between Roland and Oliver is its bitterness:[2]

> "By this beard of mine,
> If I ever see my noble sister Aude
> Again, you'll never sleep between her arms!" (CXXX)

Here the poet seems to go beyond the simple portraiture of chivalric nobility, as if he wished to reach into deeper areas of human ex-perience. He seems concerned with exploring not only a hero's com-mitment to a code, but his commitment to another human being. Oliver so loves his friend that he is willing to sacrifice his life and even his friendship to preserve that honor upon which he knows Roland's identity is founded. Oliver's wrath is an expression of charity in the extreme, medieval sense of the word, involving a concept of love for another human being where there is no self-seeking but only de-votion to the well-being of the beloved.[3] Oliver is angry, not because of any personal loss (including his life) that Roland has caused him, but only because he believes that Roland has compromised *himself*. Such notions of charitable love will abide in the male-female relation-ships of French courtly romance (at least from Chrétien de Troyes onward); and in opposition to them, the notion of concupiscent love, which is always self-seeking and evil, will normally characterize the courtly hero's rival. That Roland should be engaged to Oliver's sister gives us a sense that the theme of ideal friendship, common in heroic poetry, has been juxtaposed in a brief prophetic flash (of which we can hardly suppose the poet to have been conscious) with the theme of romantic love; thus, the ethical transition from epic to ro-mance may be less remarkable than we usually suppose.

When Oliver sees Roland's error as destruction of the bond of love between human beings, we are at the very heart of a later feudal at-titude toward social order. Human love, or charity, in the words of Saint Paul, is "the bond of perfection" between men.[4]

> Deceitfulness and injustice are inconsistent with love, the tie that was thought of as the bond of feudal society. A *vassal* was almost interchange-ably an *ami*, or, at times, a *dru*. He was bound, at least in the ideal de-manded by feudal theory, by a tie of love to his feudal overlord, and that same tie also bound his lord to him. It follows that a vassal was also bound to love his fellow-vassals. If love was the basis for the fellowship of the Church, making it, as it were, "one body" under Christ, the feudal army was also bound by a similar tie, at least in theory. "For love," as John of Salisbury wrote, "is as strong as death (Cant. 8. 6), and that battle-wedge which is bound by the bond of love is not easily broken." A Christian army ranked against heathendom could have no more appro-priate unifying principle.[5]

Oliver is angry at Roland, in other words, because his vanity has severed their relationship to their lord Charlemagne, to France, and (above all) to each other. This is indeed "love as strong as death" and expresses the essential paradox of the heroic world, that its triumph is founded on suffering and loss. An awareness of this contradiction dawns now on Oliver:

> Roland says, "What cause is there for anger?"
> And he replies, "Comrade, this is your fault.
> A vassal should love sense, instead of folly;
> And moderation counts more than excess.
> The French have died by your own recklessness.
> Never again will we serve the emperor.
> Had you believed me, our lord would have come—
> We would have won this battle here today.
> Marsile would have been taken, or even killed.
> Your courage, Roland, alas because of it!
> Charles the King will never have our aid—
> That best of men—until the judgment day.
> You shall die, and France shall be dishonored.
> Today our loyal friendship will be severed.
> By evening, we'll know the pain of parting." (CXXXI)

As we shall see, the whole tragic sense of the *Song of Roland* is related to the destruction of this bond of love which unites the Christian community in its struggles against the legions of Satan.

Since the language of the *Song of Roland* is oriented toward gestures and external realities, we are never invited to consider the inner psychological grounds for Roland's change of heart. Instead, the poet gives us actions which are at once poignant and sublime. Three *laisses similaires* depict Roland's blasts on the horn and the simultaneous responses in Charlemagne's army as the dreaded notes reach their ears. Possibly the *jongleurs* performing this poem were capable of mimetic inflections that could accommodate the tragic strains of Roland's horn as they resounded among the mountains of Ronceval:

> Roland puts the horn up to his lips.
> He holds it firmly and sounds with great force.
> High are the mountains, and the voice is long.
> Full thirty leagues away they hear its echo.
> Charlemagne hears it, and all his soldiers.
> Thus speaks the king: "Our men are waging war!" (CXXXIII)

> With pain Count Roland sounds his Oliphant.
> From his mighty effort and great anguish,

His bright blood gushes forth from his mouth.
His very brains are bursting through his temples.
He grips his horn, and its sound is mighty.
Charles hears it, as he crosses through the pass.
The Duke of Naimes and all the Frenchmen hear. . . . (CXXXIV)

Count Roland's mouth is gushing, now, with blood.
His very brains are bursting at the temples.
He sounds the Oliphant with grief and pain.
Charles hears it, and the French all listen.
Thus speaks the king: "His horn has a long sound!"
Naimes replies: "A great baron winds his pain!
There must be battle, I am sure of this.
This man has betrayed you and seeks your fall.
To arms! and let your battle cry be heard!
To the rescue of your noble household!
You've heard enough, for Roland is in pain." (CXXXV)

We can only guess, at moments like this, how far the dissociation of
the text from the music that accompanied it has impoverished us.
Here more than anywhere else we feel that a lyrical dimension prevails which the original accompaniment could only have heightened.
Music indeed subsumes action as Roland celebrates his anguish in the
full tones of his mighty horn, which the mountain setting amplifies
and echoes:

High are the mountains, and the voice is long.
Full thirty leagues away they hear its echo. (CXXXIII)

As the poet intensifies the drama of Roland's final moments, he relies
more and more upon his mountain setting to say things that are
otherwise in his idiom unsayable.[6] When Charlemagne rushes to
Roland's aid, knowing full well that he is too late, the mountains
and the valleys communicate something about the mysterious and immutable forces of which they and the fate of Roland are equally expressive:

High are the mountains, and shadowy and vast;
The valleys are deep, the waters violent.
Ahead and behind, the trumpets resound.
In unison they answer Oliphant.
The emperor rides back in great wrath,
And the French, too, in anger and grief.

> To the last man they weep in lamentations,
> And they pray that God may safeguard Roland
> Until they save him on the battlefield.
> To what avail? None. There is no hope.
> They are too late. They cannot help in time. (CXXXVIII)

As Roland himself perceives that his death is near, the outward setting becomes, for a moment, not simply expressive of, but *part* of the inner tragedy. Roland raises his eyes in anguish to the summits, as the Psalmist had done before ("I lift up my eyes to the hills. From whence does my help come? My help comes from the Lord, who made heaven and earth"):[7]

> Roland looks up to the mountains and hills.
> So many French lie dead before his eyes!
> He weeps for them, as should a noble knight:
> "Barons, Lords, may God have mercy on you!
> May he take all your souls into paradise.
> May you rest there among the holy flowers!
> Never were there vassals such as you. . . ." (CXL)

Are we at some turning point in Roland's state of mind? For a moment it seems as if Roland were on the verge of acknowledging his pride:

> "Barons of France, because of me you died.
> I cannot protect and save you now.
> May God help you, who never told a lie." (CXL)

But then, as if paralyzed by the threat of introspection, the poet plunges his hero back into the fray. He remains the willing prisoner of the externality of his idiom, and will not give Roland the self-awareness that any modern reader has come to expect as the necessary matrix of tragic experience. One critic seizes upon Roland's "because of me you died" as acknowledgment of his tragic flaw of pride (*démesure*), and I have given this idea the benefit of the doubt in my translation above. But there is every possibility that the words *pur mei* should be translated *"for me* you died," which puts the nature of Roland's self-awareness into question.[8] Surely we are mistaken if we hope to rest an eleventh-century poet's entire tragic view of things on the evidence of one very doubtful conjunction. Other critics deny altogether that the poem is tragic:

The subject of the *Chanson de Roland* is narrow, and for the men who figure in it nothing of fundamental significance is problematic. All the categories of this life and the next are unambiguous, immutable, fixed in rigid formulations. To be sure, rational comprehension has no direct access to them, but that is an observation which we ourselves make; the poem and its contemporary audience felt no such concern. They live safely and confidently in the rigid and narrow established order within which the duties of life, their distribution according to estates . . . the character of supernatural forces, and mankind's relationship thereto are regulated in the simplest way. Within this frame there are abundant and delicate emotions; there is also a certain motley variegation in external phenomena; but the frame is so restricted and rigid that properly problematic situations, let alone tragedy, can hardly arise. There are no conflicts which deserve to be called tragic.[9]

In my opinion, there are indeed grounds for calling the *Song of Roland* tragic, but not at all because Roland attains understanding of his inordinate pride. This is not a poem about spiritual metamorphosis, but about human constancy in the face of impossible odds and certain death. What is tragic in the *Song of Roland* does not involve Roland's relationship to himself, but rather his relationship to the people around him whom he loves. We shall see that as tragedy, the *Song of Roland* relies upon more than one hero for fulfillment.

Roland never loses his pride in his own excellence, but he does experience a terrible paradox: no amount of self-constancy can prevent the destruction of others around him, of people he loves as much as himself. Roland becomes vulnerable to tragedy through his attachments to other human beings. Such is the case in Homer's *Iliad* when Achilles lends his armor to Patroclus, only to have his best friend die by the sword of Hector. Such too is the case when Roland must lose his friend Oliver, not to mention the twelve peers. We may recall that earlier Roland had been confident and even exhilarated in the contemplation of martyrdom for Christ and Charlemagne:

> Thus speaks Roland: "Now we become martyrs,
> For now I see our time to live is short.
> All but cowards will sell themselves most dearly.
> Strike out, lords, with your glistening swords!
> Challenge them with both your lives and deaths,
> That sweet France may never be disgraced.
> When Charles, our Lord, returns to the field,
> He will know our treatment of the pagans

Has cost them fifteen dead for each of ours.
He shall not fail to have our bodies blessed." (CXLIV)

Now, however, Marganice (Marsile's uncle) sneaks up behind Oliver and deals him a fatal wound in the back. Oliver calls out to Roland, who rushes to his side and sees that he is dying. So great is Roland's anguish that he faints while still on horseback. The gesture is hyperbolic, to say the least, but in the context of the extraordinary which prevails in the poem it does not offend our taste. Because Oliver is too weak to recognize Roland, the poet resorts to a curious device to dramatize the bond of affection between them:

> There was Roland, fainted on his horse,
> And Oliver, standing wounded to the death.
> He had bled so much that his eyes were dim.
> He could not see enough to recognize,
> Near or far, the form of any mortal man.
> When he encountered his companion,
> He struck his helmet made of studded gold,
> And split it from the top down through the face,
> But the sword did not harm Roland's head.
> At this blow, Roland looked upon his friend:
> "Companion! did you do this by intent?
> It is I, Roland, who always loved you!
> You struck, yet never issued any challenge!"
> Oliver says, "Now I hear you speaking!
> I cannot see; may God look upon you!
> I have struck you—pardon me for this!"
> Roland replies, "No harm has come to me.
> I pardon you here and now before our God."
> At these words they lean to one another.
> Thus bound in love, the friends were cleaved apart. (CXLIX)

On an immediate level, the poet's aim to glorify Oliver here seems apparent enough. His error stems from courage that is only too perfect, and his remorse and plea for pardon reveal that he is also a perfect friend. On another level, however, we sense that the poet has asked his material to give us what it can scarcely give. A warrior is by nature a man who fights, yet our poet is attempting, with a certain boldness, to convert the apparatus of hostility into a manifestation of love. He uses a traditional formulaic sword thrust to show us what friendship is not, and then causes the two to clasp each other in grief. The most intimate moment of union between Roland and Oliver is identical with their moment of final separation.

We are involved here, perhaps, in an inherent conflict between the epic language to which the poet is committed and the sentiment that he as poet would like to convey. The warrior-ethos of his poem is splendidly equipped to portray the grandeur and horror of chivalric combat, but it allows for little purchase on other values in human life. To put it drastically, how can love be expressed with a sword? Though there is much in the *Song of Roland* that is not armor and sword, the narrative core of the poem is basically committed to destruction. The poet understands, I believe, the shortcomings of the heroic world, but he has no rhetoric of peace, love, or even friendship to mitigate its austerities. For example, Roland is engaged to Oliver's sister, yet this relationship is allowed no place in Roland's thoughts. The poet's problem is literally dramatized in the line, "Thus bound in love, the friends are cleaved apart." As we shall see later, the tragic message in the *Song of Roland* is closely involved with the poet's awareness of his material's limitations. Only with the change from epic to romance will the warrior be released from the stringencies of warfare to suffer and enjoy ("joy" is a recurrent theme in romance) the sweet pang of Cupid's arrow as opposed to the slash of the epic sword.

Despite the narrow terms of Roland's triumph, the poetry of his final moments is a high point of Western epic, most notably, perhaps, because it sustains an extraordinary balance between passion and serenity. The poet has his hero wander about the battlefield gathering up the bodies of his fallen companions, whom he lays out in rows upon the ground. Taken out of its narrative context, this episode would strain our imagination because of its improbability: not only is Roland wounded and surrounded by Saracens, but the effort of gathering up so many bodies (in full armor) would surely involve many hours of grisly labor. Such travesties of proportion are, however, the rule and not the exception in this epic, where, more than in any other, heroic action creates its own esthetic distance:

> Roland wanders about the field alone,
> Winding through the valleys and the mountains.
> Here he finds Gerin, and Gerer, his friends;
> There he finds Berenger, and Attun too,
> Anseis, Sansun, and Girard de Rossillun.
> One by one, the baron gathers them up,

And brings them all back to the archbishop.
He lays them in a row before his knees. (CLXII)

When Roland at last comes upon Oliver's body he hugs it to himself in grief, then carries it back with the rest. In this he is vainly attempting to recreate the lost fellowship of his heroic world, and once again the contradictory nature of that world is made poignantly dramatic. Only when this gruesome ritual is complete can Roland give full expression to his passion. He does so physically rather than verbally:

> Count Roland, when he sees his peers all dead,
> And Oliver, whom he loved so very much,
> Is swept with tenderness and starts to weep.
> His face is much discolored out of grief.
> So great is his grief that he cannot bear it.
> Will or nill, he falls down in a faint.
> The archbishop says: "Baron! what pity!" (CLXIV)

Roland recovers from his faint and climbs to a hilltop (once more, for reasons both dramatic and symbolic) to enact the last minutes of his life. In the words of a recent critic,

> Roland dies in solitude. Nothing distracts our attention from him. The poet composes for him a most unforgettable attitude and dramatizes it in a most unforgettable setting. Roland dies on the pedestal of a hill, in the shadow of two beautiful trees, near four shining stones, amidst a circle of high mountains. This is a contrived death, therefore, a theatrical death with supreme gestures and noble words. The poet does not wish a silent death for his hero; he wishes a death which is hortatory and triumphant, impressive and exemplary. His thoughts are full of terrestrial glory; yet the poet, by conferring upon them all possible amplitude, presents them as worthier of attention than the celestial preoccupations of Turpin. Roland is Christian, nevertheless, and in his last seconds he too will humble himself. In contrast with his friends, Roland dies in an attitude which he himself has composed. The poet went out of his way to place this scene above the rest of his work. The battlefield has vanished, and only the isolated hero remains.[10]

Deciding to break his sword rather than let it fall into the hands of someone "who might flee before another," Roland strikes Durendal on a stone. But instead of splintering, the sword proudly springs back toward the sky. The sword "projects" in this way the spirit of Roland the warrior, and though Roland himself is fading quickly, the spectacle of his own honor embodied in a noble weapon elicits from him a formulaic hero's response, now familiar to the audience, which assures us that Roland's spirit is undaunted. An instant's flash of sunlight on steel calls to mind an entire lifetime of heroic deeds:

> "Ah, Durendal! How fine and clear and white!
> How you shine and flame out in the sunlight!
> Charles was in the valley of Maurienne
> When God sent an angel with the command
> That you should pass into the hands of a count.
> Then he girded me with you, that gentle king.
> I conquered Anjou, also Brittany;
> I conquered Poitou, Normandy, and Maine. . . ." (CLXXII)

The merits that Roland attributes to his God-given weapon are also his own. Without losing its value as the conventional symbol of Christian fortitude, the sword incorporates Roland's very self as his life passes in review. In this poem, the mediation of the physical world is necessary, it seems, even if one wishes to have access to one's own thoughts. The list of Durendal's achievements is not merely a testimony of self-satisfaction, but the attempt of a dying hero to reconstitute his own personality in a final, monumental form. This is less a moment of transfiguration than of expansion in a feudal, aristocratic consciousness.

Roland's last breaths are spent in prayer. Three times he strikes his chest in penitence, yet he never reveals exactly what sins he has in mind. Does Roland repent of his *démesure,* as some critics believe? We do not know—verbalization of inner motives in this poem is scant, as we have seen. Perhaps a clue to Roland's conception of himself is to be found in his allusions to God's salvation of Lazarus and Daniel: Lazarus represents resurrection, and Daniel is an example of defiant faith; both were innocent men when they died. However, whereas Roland's words reveal little of his state of mind, his last gestures reveal a great deal. From his face turned toward the enemy (Spain) we know that he dies unvanquished in spirit; from his position on his side, striking his chest, we know that he dies penitent; from his memories, we know that he dies a loyal Frenchman; from his joined hands and extended glove, we know that he dies a Christian and a true vassal of God. Saints Gabriel and Michael, each a patron saint of chivalry, descend and bear his soul up to Paradise:

Roland the count lay down beneath a pine.
Back toward Spain he turned his face,
While many things passed through his memory,
How many lands he had conquered as a knight,
Sweet France, and the image of his kinsmen,
Charlemagne, his lord, who nourished him;
He cannot hold back his tears and his sighs.
He does not forget himself, however,
Confessing his faults and praying God for grace:
"True father, who never lied to man,
Who resurrected Lazarus from death,
And rescued Daniel from the lion's den,
Now protect my soul from every peril
Of sins that I committed in this world!"
Roland extends his right glove up to God.
Saint Gabriel now takes it from his hand.
His head is now at rest upon his arm.
His hands are clasped as he goes to his end.
God sends down his angel Cherubin
In company with Saint Michel del Peril;
Together with them comes Saint Gabriel.
They bear the count's soul up to Paradise. (CLXXVXL)

As a character, Roland is so commanding that he has progressively effaced all the other important characters in the first half of the poem. When it began, the *Song of Roland* had the appearance of a predominately social epic, for first, individual personalities were woven into a complex fabric of personal and political relationships. One by one, however, its characters, as well as the perspectives that they offered, have vanished; now we are face to face with a solitary human being, far from the hue and cry of the battlefield, in an artificially tranquil, meditative setting. No other hero in the epic tradition ends his days in such total seclusion as Roland. Where did all those Saracens go?

Perhaps the direction of the narrative in the Oxford version reflects what will be a growing tendency in twelfth-century thought to move away from the norms of collective, public experience in order to grasp the quality of what is distinctive in an individual's experience. The epic hero is a leader of men, but the hero of romance is essentially a solitary figure, at least during major portions of his ordeal. In the *Song of Roland,* armor and weapons serve as an extension of the warrior's personality into the material world; but in romances such as Chrétien's *Yvain,* armor tends to conceal a man from society, to isolate his identity, and to delineate the private from the public man. During the twelfth century, there was an increasing tendency for the dialectic of the literary battlefield to move inward into the mind, to become psychological rather than physical.[11] Dialogue, moreover, tends to replace physical action. This is true of the Grail literature, which converted chivalric romance into spiritual allegory; this is especially true of the thirteenth-century *Romance of the Rose,* whose setting is wholly enclosed within the dreamer's imagination and whose action is primarily verbal. Correspondingly, in religious thought, Saint Bernard, the Cistercian abbot of Clairvaux, tended to de-emphasize aspects of collective spirituality in the Rule of Saint Benedict and to cultivate acts of mystical meditation within the individual, leading to ecstasy and union of the soul with God. Wherever one looks in twelfth-century letters, one notices an increasing urge in men to fulfill themselves by inward actions of the soul.

Because the artistic resources of the feudal epic were better prepared to deal with the more outward, conventional aspects of human behavior than with the subjective, the best way for a poet to approach the individual would be to create a privileged physical setting which would pertain exclusively to that individual's state of mind: hence, the restrictive privacy of Roland's final moments, where the inner and the outer man become almost indistinguishable. Indeed, at the moment when Roland dies, his spiritual self is so completely objectified that it figures in the narrative like any other object: Gabriel and Michael descend and physically bear Roland's soul up into the sky.

Like any other period in history, however, the twelfth century had its contradictions. Hence, if there was one tendency toward a detachment of the individual from collective experience, there was another tendency—just as marked—toward consolidation of the individual into corporate social forms. This latter impulse can be felt in the trend toward strong national monarchies in Europe, and locally, in the constitution of communes, the foundation of guilds, and in the establishment of new religious organisms, including universities. No doubt, Roland's personal virtuosity appealed to a twelfth-century audience; at the same time, to an audience of that "second feudal age" (as Marc Bloch calls it), when an urge for unity and political stability made itself apparent, his social conduct must have posed real problems. As a social creature, Roland incarnates (as does the Anglo-Saxon hero Byrhtnoth in "The Battle of Malden") the virtues of a crude, warlike society, which adored military valor to the exclusion of almost all other virtues.[12] The poet gives himself unstintingly to this Roland during the first half of the epic, but the ethical viewpoints represented by Oliver and Charlemagne, as well as the judicial question negatively raised by Ganelon, are far too important to remain buried permanently behind Roland's magnificence. Bédier, whose real interest lay in the first half of the poem, asks about Roland and the twelve peers,

> Would their lord and "sweet France" have gained more if they had grown old, like old Naimes? Or is it better that a "good song" has been sung of them? Between "boldness" and "discretion" our poet has not chosen; he was too human to choose.[13]

Too human to choose? Perhaps. But he was also too human not to reconsider. I am convinced that the poet saw Roland's ordeal as part of a larger social dilemma involving the conflict of interests between the crown and the chief nobility of France, analogous in one respect to the conflict between federalism and states' rights in the United States. An eleventh-century audience could only have been sensitive to the problems generated by Roland's destructive individualism, to the point where the poet's pride as a *jongleur* must have compelled him to elaborate on issues that had become central to society with the passing of time. The premises of the oral epic, like those of any art, are subject to change. Hence, we have a second half of the *Song of Roland.* Roland's memory persists; but now the hero is undeniably Charlemagne. Between the two heroes a tragic theme evolves, which separately neither could have sustained. We must take up this question in the ensuing chapters.

⊰ VI ⊱

ROLAND, CHARLEMAGNE, AND
TRAGIC PERSPECTIVE

Roland's is a tale of triumph, but is not by itself tragic. True, we are
swept with the majesty of his final gestures, but as Roland looks
back in time from the edge of death, he never comes to terms with
his own human limitations or with the destruction that his pride has
inflicted upon the rest of society. Roland achieves a kind of perfection,
but it is too autistic. Whatever understanding of mortality he begins
to derive from his suffering is quickly offset by the joy of his apotheosis
when Gabriel and Saint Michael bear his soul up to heaven. This is
exalted Christian comedy.

The poet, however, does not share for long the serenity of his hero,
but with an urgent *non sequitur,* deflects the locus of his narrative
downward in a single poetic line from the glorious heights of heaven
to the ruined community of mortals who must suffer the consequences
of Ganelon's treason and—just as importantly—of Roland's pride. The
narrative now centers on Charlemagne, who is caught in a tempest of
grief and who struggles to grasp the enormity of his loss in ritualized
lamentations based on the unanswerable question one must ask about
all things of this transitory world: *ubi est?*

> Roland is dead; God has his soul in heaven.
> The emperor returns to Ronceval.
> There is no roadway, patch, or path of land
> Whose every foot of every mile does not
> Contain dead Frenchmen, or else Saracens.
> Charles cries: "Where are you, beautiful nephew?
> Where is the archbishop? and Count Oliver?
> Where is Gerins? and Garers, his companion?
> Where is Otes? And the Count Berenger?
> Ive and Ivorie, whom I loved so dearly?
> What happened to the Gascon, Engeler?
> Sansun the Duke? and Baron Anseis?

Where is Girard de Russillun le Veilz?
Where are the twelve peers, whom I left behind?"
What use is it, when they do not answer?
"Lord!" says the king, "What cause I have to grieve!
Had I but been there at the battle's start!"
He tears his beard like a man in anguish;
His barons and his knights weep at the eyes.
Twenty thousand others faint to the ground.
The Duke of Naimes is swept with violent pity. (CLXXVII)

The center has dropped out of the heroic world. We are left with a man two hundred years old who not only is beyond action but has lost everyone he loved most in the world. Because Charlemagne loves human beings more than heroes, he can find no consolation in Roland's hard-won glory to balance the loss of his nephew. Aside from the personal loss, moreover, there is a severe strategic loss for Charlemagne: "The flower of France" has been ravished, and twenty thousand of his best knights are dead.

As the new hero of the *Song of Roland,* Charlemagne represents a perspective of disillusionment with those heroic values for which Roland lived and died. True, this perspective has been latent in the poem since the first council scene, yet neither Charlemagne nor Oliver has been allowed to eclipse Roland's heroic achievement. Though the most powerful man in the world, Charlemagne has remained passive throughout the poem; as for Oliver, he was never granted the stature, necessary for a true hero, of influencing the course of events in the slightest degree. With the new hero—who this time is an old man—comes a shift of emphasis in the narrative. True, the tale almost recovers its earlier narrative tempo when Charlemagne takes revenge upon the Saracens, yet the poet no longer exults in the splendid battle rituals of before. Without the right hero, there is no real action. Instead, the poet miraculously (and conveniently) disposes of the pagan army in the river Ebro and brings the focus of his poem back to Charles, for whom this abbreviated victory brings no joy:

For Charlemagne God showed his mighty power;
He caused the sun to stand completely still.
The pagans flee, the French in hot pursuit.
They catch them in the Vale of Shadows
And drive them fiercely toward Saragossa,
Killing them all the way with mighty blows.

> They cut off all the major roads and paths.
> Only the Ebro's waters wait for them,
> Very deep and marvelous and fast.
> There is no barge or boat of any kind,
> The pagans call in prayer to Tervagant,
> Then jump; but nothing can protect them.
> Those who wear knight's armor weigh the most,
> And sink to the bottom in great numbers.
> Others float, and drift off in the current.
> The luckiest drink their fill from the first,
> But all are finally drowned with marvelous cries.
> The Frenchmen cry, "Roland, alas for you!" (CLXXX)

As soon as the business of revenge is complete, grief overtakes the
Frenchmen in the form of utter exhaustion. Charlemagne lies down to
sleep in full armor; even the horses are too tired to stand, but must
graze lying down. This nocturnal scene of prostration is the poetic
antithesis of those earlier daylight scenes where armies stood eager to
attack:

> The night is clear, and the moon shines brightly.
> Charles lies down, but still he grieves for Roland.
> For Oliver, too, whose death weighs upon him,
> For the twelve peers and the noble Frenchmen,
> Who suffered bloody deaths at Ronceval.
> He cannot stint his tears and lamentations,
> And prays to God that all their souls be saved.
> He falls asleep, now, out of sheer exhaustion.
> Frenchmen lie asleep in every field.
> Not one horse can remain on its feet:
> Those who wish grass must eat it lying down.
> A man has learned much who has suffered much. (CLXXV)

A hero is dead, and a poem of energy and action is conspicuously
still. Earlier, in Roland's world, life had an eager buoyancy, and
death seemed like nothing more than a release of heroic energy as
stout souls hurled themselves from this life into the next. Death was
everywhere, yet it was nowhere. Now, however, death takes on a more
somber dimension. Through their devotion to Roland, whom they
have lost, Charlemagne and the French barons learn the full consequences of death as a tragic fact of human existence. Roland's death
is now the central event of the world, and the poet has measured the

full meaning of this event by bringing the heroic world to an elegiac standstill: day has turned into night, joy into grief, energy into exhaustion, and most significantly, courage into wisdom; as the poet says, "He has learned much who has suffered much."

As Charlemagne sleeps, he experiences prophetic dreams which prefigure the two main events of the story still to follow: the so-called "Baligant episode" and the trial of Ganelon. Then the poet directs his attention to the pagan world, and devotes an interlude of 275 lines to the Saracens as they prepare for new and larger war with the Christians. The narrative discontinuity between episodes has led many critics to suspect that the story of Baligant is a late interpolation into the tale of Roland and Charlemagne. I shall reserve this question for the next chapter, and shall move forward in the present discussion to that point where Charlemagne awakes and returns to Ronceval to honor the bodies of his fallen nephew and the twelve peers.

The moment when Charlemagne discovers Roland's body is perhaps the most moving of the whole poem. Meticulously composed, this scene exploits in vivid and dramatic terms a contrast of perspectives upon the heroic world that has grown out of the presence of two central heroes—one old, one young—in a single tale. Here more than anywhere else the poet concentrates his narrative resources to deepen the meaning of the disaster at Ronceval, and he achieves thereby what might be considered the finest tragic moment in all feudal literature.

No lesser figure is allowed to intrude upon the intimacy of that instant when Charlemagne finds his nephew's body:

> Charlemagne arrives at Ronceval.
> He starts to weep at the dead men he sees,
> And says to the French, "Lords, hold back your pace,
> For I myself must go before you all.
> I alone must come upon my nephew.
> When I was at a solemn feast at Aix,
> And my bold knights were boasting of their deeds,
> Of their great battles and their bold assaults,
> I heard Roland say that he would never die
> In a strange realm unless he fought much further
> Into enemy land than all his men.
> His head would be turned to face the enemy."
> He led them by a stone's throw and climbed the hill. (CCIV)

That the poet should single out Charlemagne to discover Roland's body is important to the unity of his poem: Roland and Charlemagne are supreme in the warrior's ethos and share in a single identity, except that one is young and bold, the other old and wise. Charlemagne alone is worthy both to grasp the full meaning of Roland's final acts and to appraise them in a perspective of tragic wisdom which the young warrior himself could never achieve.

The approach to Roland's body is presented through Charlemagne's eyes, and once again we move in a landscape suffused with human expressiveness:

> While the emperor hunted for his nephew,
> He saw countless flowers in the fields,
> Stained all crimson with our barons' blood.
> He could not stop from weeping out of pity.
> He came to a place beneath two trees,
> And saw the blood of Roland on three stones.
> On the green grass he found his nephew lying.
> It is no wonder that he felt great pain.
> He left his horse and went to Roland running.
> Between his two hands [he clasped his nephew]
> And fainted over him, such was his anguish.[1] (CCV)

The flowers stained with the blood of his favorite warriors convey in a single image the idea of vernal (and perhaps regenerative) beauty combined with the pathos of youth cut down in its very prime. Our poet has hit here upon an antithesis that has been indigenous to epic poetry ever since the *Iliad*; indeed, this is a permanent truth of the warrior's world.[2] The contradictory aspect of blood on flowers mirrors a contradiction in Charlemagne's own mind, for he is capable, by virtue of his own heroism and his supreme old age, of perceiving both the glory of heroic martyrdom and its tragedy. The association of the bloodied flowers and "our barons" is strengthened by Charlemagne's reference to his barons elsewhere in the poem as the "flower of France," and by his prayer that his barons should rest among the "holy flowers" of the saved in paradise.

When Charlemagne revives from his faint, he begins a complaint (*planctus*) which is sustained through the next five *laisses*. The *planctus* is a conventional resource of French epic and comprises an *ensemble* of recognizable formulas. Of the six complaints uttered by warriors grieving for dead companions in the *Song of Roland*, Charlemagne's is the longest and summarizes the motifs of all the previous complaints.[3] Charlemagne's first utterance is short and shows the extent to which he identifies his nephew's heroic glory with his own:

> "Roland, friend, may God have mercy on you!
> Never did a man see such a knight
> Engage in mighty battles, joust, and win.
> My honor is beginning to decline."
> Charlemagne faints; he cannot prevent it. (CCVI)

Though gestures in the *Song of Roland* have an irreducible simplicity about them, I am tempted to see the "epic faint" as a symbolic, vicarious death which a hero experiences at the loss of someone he loves as much as himself. Both Roland, who fainted when Oliver died, and Charlemagne, who faints now, proclaim that grief has made of life an unwelcome burden. As the emperor regains consciousness, he contemplates Roland's body—as I have said, the basis for emotions in a hero is always rooted in the exterior world. Roland in death expresses something he could never express in life: his body retains both the beauty of his youth and the tragic darkness of death. Shadows in the *Song of Roland* have repeatedly suggested death, and now the shadows are located in Roland's very eyes:

> Charlemagne the king came out of his faint.
> Four of his barons hold him up by the hands.
> He looks to the ground where his nephew lies.
> His body is splendid, but now is pale.
> His eyes are turned up, and are shadowy.
> Charles weeps for him in faith and love. (CCVII)

Through the mediation of Charlemagne we understand that the triumph of chivalric honor, still discernible in the posture of Roland's remains, is founded upon suffering and death. This is the supreme paradox of the heroic warrior's world, and it now stands revealed with stark but monumental simplicity. What earlier was Christian comedy has veered toward tragedy.

In his second soliloquy, Charlemagne elaborates upon his grief, exclaiming that with Roland, a part of himself has died. He even goes so far as to blame himself for Roland's death—why, we are not told. We may only surmise that he reproaches himself for not having intervened in the course of events to protect his nephew: protection (*warrantia*), after all, is a feudal lord's obligation to his vassal:

"Roland, friend, may your soul rest among flowers
In paradise, among the glorious.
What a bad lord you followed into Spain!
There will be no day when I do not grieve.
How my force is fading, and my courage!
No one remains to hold up my honor:
I think I have no friend beneath the sky;
There are relatives, but none is so bold."
He tears his hair with both hands together;
One hundred thousand Frenchmen feel such grief
That every single one is weeping hard. AOI (CCVII)

Charlemagne is a warrior who has inherited all the tragic consequences of the warrior's way of life and death. As king of the Franks, his fate has subsumed that of his vassals. Yet the quality of the world in this poem is such that it can offer him no consolation. He experiences the tragedy of a whole ethos, and perhaps even of a poetic genre. Charlemagne's lament extends not only to the fallen hero, and to himself, but to a whole beloved order that is now irretrievably lost:

"Ah, France, now you are left empty!
So great is my grief, I wish I were no more."
He begins to tear at his white beard,
And with both hands tears hair from his head.
A hundred thousand Frenchmen faint to the ground. (CCIX)

Nothing meaningful remains in the world, and Charlemagne, like Achilles when he weeps for Patroclus, wants only to die so that he may rejoin his friends in both body and soul:

May God grant, and Saint Mary's Son,
That my soul be set free from my body
Before I cross the pass of Cize today,
And that I be placed among their souls,
While my flesh is buried here with theirs. (CCX)

But Charlemagne is denied the tranquility that Roland enjoyed at his death. He seems to be caught in the hell of his own role and cannot die.

The scene of lamentation completes a shift of emphasis between the poem's two major voices, for the *Song of Roland* has at last become Charlemagne's. Roland's memory will endure to the end of the poem, but Charlemagne provides a context of wisdom and maturity in which the consequences of Roland's ordeal and passion take on their full meaning. Although with the unfolding of time the psychological outline of neither Roland nor Charlemagne has changed, we of the audience have experienced a profound reversal of perspective, which carries us beyond the arrogant pride of a young knight to the tragic wisdom of supreme old age. A tragedy of personalities is virtually complete now, yet the poet continues. Why? Has the narrative run away with itself? Is there some deeper, unfulfilled purpose which drives the poet to spin new movements, like a symphonic composer? These are questions of poetic intention, impossible to resolve, impossible to resist, and they will preoccupy us next.

⤳ VII ⤫

THE BALIGANT EPISODE

Although I believe that it has the character of a work unified by a single poetic talent, the *Song of Roland* is only one member of a whole cycle of poems about Charlemagne. Hindsight, at least, has borne this out, for we know more about sequels to the poem than antecedents.[1] The *chanson de geste* was originally a kind of improvised poetry that survived by changing, and the Oxford version of Roland's story was artificially arrested when it was detached from the environment of oral poetry and "fixed" by an individual poet or scribe on parchment. The Oxford manuscript is like a photograph of moving water where, for all its clarity, immobility is an illusion. From the poor quality of the parchment, moreover, it is apparent that the book itself, the book as object, had no particular significance to the poem it contained as a creative work. In fact, the impulse to attach symbolic meaning to the book as object remained peculiar to the sacred and learned tradition of medieval Latin until the thirteenth century; only then were these ideas vernacularized. So, when a scribe set this poem down on parchment, he did not have any sense of appropriating eternal fame for himself.[2] The poetic legend continued to be anonymous; hence, the property of all. The *Song of Roland,* even in this manuscript, is less poetry as *product* than poetry as *process,* a continuation among continuations.

Never is the modern reader of the *Song of Roland* more likely to fear that the poem is only on arbitrary compilation than when the poet deserts the narrows of Ronceval and the exalted crescendos of passion in Roland and Charlemagne to launch into a phlegmatic and seemingly unrelated episode which records the demise of Baligant, the Babylonian emir. We hear of Baligant for the first time in *laisse* CLXXXIX, when we suddenly learn that Marsile has been imploring Baligant for aid during the seven years of Charlemagne's campaign in Spain, but that Baligant only now has decided to rally to the support of his defeated ally. Occupying more than a quarter of the total of the *Roland* text, the so-called "Baligant episode" includes a long chronicle-like list of battle-corps from both sides (the French have ten, the Saracens no less than thirty), a rather pale description of a combat between them, and a compressed narration of a duel between Charlemagne and Baligant, which can be described as little more than epic shorthand.

To say the least, the Baligant episode inaugurates a wholly different poetic climate in the *Song of Roland*. The violent antitheses of the mountain setting in the Pyrenees, so appropriate to the intimate expression of Roland's tragedy, now dilate into a wide-open space where large-scale, impersonal armies conduct the least inventive feudal warfare imaginable. "Broad is the plain, the land is wide open"—such space without contours accommodates a human world similarly without contours; gone is the resounding extravagance of joy and despair which orchestrates the poem's first half. Why, critics ask, should Baligant make what seems to be a gratuitous entry into the *Song of Roland*? What relationship is there between the Baligant episode and the events that precede and follow it?

Some critics have deemed the Baligant episode the contamination of some lesser poet's hand and have accordingly banished it from their editions of the poem.[3] Other critics, by contrast, vibrating with polemical joy, assert that the Baligant episode and the rest of the *Roland* form an altogether harmonious whole.[4] My own instinct as a reader is to feel that neither extreme is justified and that if we stay on middle ground we will discover subtle artistic problems that finally deepen the message of the *Song of Roland* more than they confuse it.

We have already seen in earlier chapters that even during Roland's half of the epic, the poet sustains a current of *malaise* that counteracts any complacency about the values of the heroic code rooted in the narrative tradition behind the poem. By the time the Oxford version of the poem was composed, shadows were lengthening in the heroic world, and despite Roland's *brio* and magnificence, his tale must have vexed a late eleventh-century audience as well as pleased it. It is as true of the *chanson de geste* as of any art that material inherited from a tradition will inevitably seem problematic and unbalanced to the poet and audience of a new generation. If the oral poem does not adapt itself, it quickly falls into oblivion. Thus, the variants of the *chanson de geste* are to some extent dictated by the perpetual inappropriateness of the material of one age to another. The tenuous relationship of the Baligant episode to the poem as a whole suggests that this poet was highly sensitive to certain crucial complexities of his historical age.

However triumphant it is, the story of Roland's ordeal leaves us with an image of a Charlemagne who is profoundly humiliated as a person, as a leader, and as a Christian. We see him weak and indecisive, even, before the quarrels among his vassals, strategically unwise in assigning his twelve peers and his best knights to the exposed command of the rearguard, and outrageously tricked by a depraved pagan enemy, an enemy of God. Such humiliation almost demands, in literature, that redemption follow, and the existence of the story's second half, which deals with Charlemagne, suggests that such a compulsion was strong in the mind of our poet—at least of *some* poet. This is easily explained. Many of the leaders of later feudalism looked back at Charlemagne with nostalgia and veneration. Not only had he been king of the Franks, but he had represented as well the continuity of imperial Rome, the fourth monarchy prophesied by Daniel (2:39–40) which was to have endured *in finem saeculi*—that is, until the final struggle with the anti-Christ should usher in the millennium of Christ, the fifth and final monarchy. A memory of the Carolingian Empire persisted as a dream of universalism during those three centuries of political chaos that followed it, during which time (particularly in France) political power became hopelessly fragmented among the feuding nobility.[5] Charlemagne was also celebrated as a tireless defender of the Christian faith, whose conquests were said to have thrown back the boundaries of paganism and to have worked innumerable conversions. During the centuries after his reign, Charlemagne's legend gathered prestige in liturgy and chronicles pertaining to him, especially in Germany, where imperial sentiment remained high, to the point that Frederick I attempted to have him canonized at Aachen (Aix) in 1165.[6] Charlemagne's legendary virtues were brought to bear on the crusaders of 1095, when Pope Urban II said in one of his sermons to Christ's athletes as they were preparing to set forth:

> May the acts of your ancestors excite and stir up your souls, and the prowess and magnificence of King Charlemagne and of his son Louis and of your other kings who have destroyed the pagan kingdom at the boundaries of the Holy Church. . . . Oh, most bold knights, you, the

fruit of invincible lineages, do not become degenerate, but think of the valor of your fathers! [7]

The insertion of the Baligant episode in the *Roland* may be understood as one poet's commentary on the tale of Roland in the light of later social attitudes. A story of blind temerity, the first half of the *Song of Roland* could doubtless still appeal to an eleventh-century audience as a monument to a glorious age still within memory; nevertheless, as an expression of contemporary needs, it fell short and challenged the poet to an extension. Thus the Baligant episode and the trial of Ganelon (which I shall discuss later) may both be regarded as responses to cultural attitudes in Capetian France which inspired men to emphasize those aspects of legendary history that could enhance the hope of achieving some kind of political stability in the world. Even though Roland's death is already avenged before the Baligant episode, the poet probably wished to revive an image of Charlemagne enjoying the full prestige that his memory could still evoke at the end of the eleventh century. Accordingly, a need arose in the poem for an antagonist of Charlemagne's own stature, one who could pretend to the same universalism as Charlemagne himself. With the arrival of Baligant, the ideological axis of the poem no longer involves just France and Moslem Spain, but East and West.

However we may account for it, the poet's decision to revive the image of Charlemagne in the Baligant episode gives rise to some artistic cross-purposes. During the first half of the poem, the tragic contradictions of the heroic world find expression in the dialectic of personalities. Now, however, we have two contrary values expressed in a *single* hero, Charlemagne. The poet asks a figure who is spiritually and physically exhausted to assume a hero's role as Christ's vicar in the struggle against the legions of Satan. Yet this same figure's sole present desire is to leave the burdens of this life and to be united with his barons in Paradise. Needless to say, one side of Charlemagne's character cannot conceivably flourish except at the expense of the other, especially since the poet's narrative resources do not lend themselves well to exploring psychological conflicts in his characters.

The gravity of the poet's artistic cross-purposes becomes all too evident when we analyze the substance of his narrative. The Baligant episode is some 1,228 verses long. Only 190 of these are devoted to the actual battle between the two armies, and only 64 are devoted to the climactic duel between Charlemagne and Baligant, which (like the duel between Aeneas and Turnus in Virgil's epic), is to settle the war. In other words, what ought to have been the dramatic focal point in the second half of the *Song of Roland* turns out to be, epically, a narrative flop. The poet devotes a quarter of the whole episode to a mere chronicle-like list of the troops who are to participate. Although an epic "who's who" of the Carolingian Empire could flatter an ancestor-conscious audience in the eleventh century, it brings the narrative to a standstill. Heroes are named everywhere but act nowhere! From the poverty of invention here and the tritely formulaic description of the duel between Charlemagne and Baligant, we suspect that the poet may be as weary of the heroic world as Charlemagne himself. Instead of taking the trouble to differentiate between his characters, for example, he invites us to see double, as if a single knight fought against himself in a mirror:

> French and pagans both strike with their swords.
> What noble barons lead them into battle!
> Neither one forgets his battle cry:
> "Precious!" cries out the emir: that was his cry.
> Charlemagne answers with his own: "Munjoie!"
> They know each other by their high, clear voices.
> They meet each other in the battlefield,
> And begin to strike, exchanging mighty blows,
> With swords that fall upon the rounded shields.
> They break them over the heavy buckles.
> They cut away the rings upon their mail,
> But do not harm the flesh contained within.
> Then the cinches break and the saddles turn.
> The two kings fall, but spin around again
> And quickly rise upon their feet once more.
> Again, the noble vassals draw their swords.
> Never will this battle draw to a close,
> Until one of these men is struck down dead. (CCLVIII)

If the poet nods during the battles of the Baligant episode, there are other moments, nevertheless, when he achieves some remarkably fresh effects. These tend to be clustered in his descriptions of the Saracen people. Nominally, at least, the cleavage of the world in the *Song of Roland* into opposing camps dramatizes broad moral conflicts between good and evil, Christianity and paganism, loyalty and treachery, as they were perceived by a pious mind at the end of the

eleventh century. Yet there are times when we feel that the poet of
the *Song of Roland* is more artist than moralist, which is to say that
his mind accepts the polarized framework of his cultural world without, however, denying the urge to explore what is taboo. Like Tasso
and Spenser, our poet is curious about the operations and attractions
of evil, and the forbidden world occasions some of his best poetry.
Theologically, of course, there was no place for doubt as a moral tool
in the prelogical, crusading mind of the eleventh century; yet curiosity
itself (as medieval moralists were well aware) can be a form of doubt
and can defy the restraints of moral categories without overtly break-
ing out of them. The Saracen world satisfies all the direst criteria for
evil but seems to satisfy, as well, a taste for the exotic and for sensuous
delight. One wonders, indeed, if the *Roland* does not betray a certain
ambivalence of motive which the crusaders shared—those of them
who came back from the East. For the Saracens are most damnably
worldly. They love gold, jewelry, fine silk, and gorgeous colors. When
Marsile wishes to bribe Charlemage into returning to Aix, the gifts
he proposes are sumptuous: bears, lions, dogs, 700 camels, 1000 freshly
molted falcons, 400 mules loaded with gold and silver, 50 wagons
full of money. Again, when Marsile decides not to slay Ganelon during the stormy embassy scene, he offers a huge treasure of sables,
which Ganelon accepts—the wages of sin can be elegant! Moreover,
Arab worldliness includes a strong penchant for the arts of civiliza-
tion: Marsile sits on a throne of blue marble; Baligant sits on a throne
of ivory, before which is spread a great rug of white silk; Abisme carries
a shield (given him, as we have noted, by a devil) studded with
amethysts, topazes, and carbuncles which "flame" in the light; Anseis's
shield is of vermillion and azure. All this Saracen finery is seen at its
most brilliant at the instant when it is destroyed. On such instants
the poet dwells again and again, as the sword of virtue shatters a
precious work of pagan art. Here, for example, is Oliver's sword bringing down Justin de Val Feree:

> He splits the whole head right down the middle.
> He cleaves the body and the saffron-colored mail.
> And the beautiful saddle in gemmed gold. (CVII)

And then bringing down Marganice:

> He holds Halteclere, whose steel is brown,
> And strikes Marganice on the helmet, pointed
> And made of gold; flowers and crystals shatter. (CXLVI)

In the second instance Oliver "shakes the sword in the wound and knocks him dead." But the triumph of morality only highlights the beauty of earthly wealth by destroying it in an explosion of light and color. Does the poet mourn or exult? Consider too the description of Baligant's fleet as it sets sail for Spain in darkness, casting all the while a sinister glow:

> They set sail and row, their rudders on course.
> From atop the masts and from the high bows
> Shine forth many carbuncles and lanterns.
> From above, they cast forward such a glow
> That in the night the sea is beautiful.
> When they come to the Spanish mainland,
> The whole country is lit up, and shines. . . .
> They leave the sea and sail in fresh water;
> They pass by Marbrise and they pass by Marbrose,
> And slink up the Ebro with all their ships,
> Shining with countless lights and carbuncles,
> Which give great clarity throughout the night.
> At dawn they arrive at Saragossa. (CXC–CXCI)

Though passages of such visual beauty are rare in the *Song of Roland,* they give rise to an ambivalence that is discernible in other highly charged moral epics, such as the *Aeneid,* the *Gerusalemme liberata,* and the *Faerie Queene:* the artist in the poet often clings to what the moralist must put away.

The poet of the *Roland* finds material in Saracen culture to cloy the ear, as well as the eye. Evocative names, like "Escababi," for example, are sometimes marshalled into resonant lists like this inventory of Baligant's battle corps, bristling with French xenophobia but filled with intimations of a world both fearful and inviting:

> The first is of men from Butentrot . . .
> And next, those from Miscenes, with their big heads;
> And the third comes from Nubles and from Blos,
> And the fourth from Bruns and Esclavoz,
> And the fifth is from Sorbres and from Sorz,
> And the sixth is from Ermines and Mors,
> And the seventh is from Jericho,
> And the eighth is from Nigre, the ninth from Gros,
> And the tenth comes from Balide the Strong. (CCXXXII)

The sensuality of the pagan world is characteristic of its leaders as well. Not once does the poet describe Roland or Oliver, yet Baligant is portrayed in considerable detail and favorably combines the attributes of both age and youth:

> The baron is very strong in his thighs;
> His flanks are narrow, his rib cage broad.
> His chest is huge and finely sculptured.
> His shoulders are strong and his face is clear.
> His look is proud, his head has a crop of hair,
> As white as a flower in the summertime. (CCXXVIII)

The poet bestows on Baligant a supreme compliment by wishing what we all wish at times, that evil were good:

> God, what a baron! If only Christian! (CCXXVIII)

The gorgeousness of the Saracens' attire makes them effeminate in appearance, but (as the whole poem shows) they are strong fighters nonetheless. Baligant's shield, for instance, has a buckle of gold and is bordered with crystal. The strap is fashioned of the best silk, embroidered with circles. His sword's name is "Precieuse," and "Precieuse!" is the cry of his men as they rush into battle.

It is primarily through such contrasts that the Christian and pagan worlds define each other. What a difference between battle cries: "Munjoie!" (Mount-Joy?) and "Precieuse!" One suggests joy won through hardship—perhaps even through crucifixion; the other is absurd and insolent, suggesting vain mockery of virtue. The relation of evil to good here is that of demonic parody, and may well be the poet's extension of fundamental medieval attitudes toward a world created by a benevolent God who nonetheless accommodates evil. As St. Augustine had said in his *City of God*:

> . . . even the wicked will is a strong proof of the goodness of the nature. But God, as he is the supremely good Creator of good natures, so is He of evil wills the most just Ruler; so that, while they make an ill use of good natures, He makes a good use even of evil wills. Accordingly, He caused the devil (good by God's creation, wicked by his own will) to be cast down from his high position, and to become the mockery of His angels—that is, He caused his temptations to benefit those whom He wishes to injure by them.[8]

St. Augustine even makes an analogy between the dialectical quality of good poetry and the dialectic of history in which man may exercise free will in the choice of good or evil:

As, then, these oppositions of contraries lend beauty to the language, so the beauty of the course of this world is achieved by the opposition of contraries, arranged, as it were, by an eloquence not of words, but of things. This is quite plainly stated in the *Book of Ecclesiasticus* [33:15] this way: "Good is set against evil and life against death: so is the sinner against the godly. So look upon all the works of the Most High, and these are two and two, one against another." [9]

What I find most interesting about the Baligant episode is that the absolute, established categories of good and evil appear to be eroding before our eyes: moral triumph becomes unrewarding and dull, and pretended pagan depravity vibrates with all the colors of life. The moral framework of the poem remains intact, to be sure, yet we can only feel that the impulse to censure is equalled by the impulse to innovate and explore. I am convinced that the *Song of Roland* is a poem whose premises change profoundly as continuations are added, and that the outlook imparted at the end is radically different from that at the beginning. It is interesting to observe, moreover, that many of the vices of the Saracen world—the love of finery, of what is sumptuously stylized, even of life itself—become virtues, within a generation or two, in the world of romance. It is dangerous to read history backwards, but I find it interesting to note, as well, that the only woman of consequence in the *Roland* is Bramimonde, the wife of Marsile, who is both attractive and loyal, and whom the poet elects to redeem at the poem's end by conversion. Perhaps we would not be wrong to speculate that the Baligant episode, with its unplanned failures and successes, emblemizes an artist's dilemma, a conflict of values, which will be happily resolved only with the new creative outlets of romance.

Whether or not these thoughts capture anything of the true significance of the Baligant episode, I remain convinced that its presence in the *Song of Roland* raises problems that are complex but instructive. Weak spots in poetry can provide valuable critical insights, and we sometimes owe them the same kind of consideration that we devote to passages of special artistic merit. True, subsequent versions of the *Song of Roland* omit the Baligant episode; but then, none of these later poets achieves anything of the power of this earliest *chanson de geste:* why, therefore, should we accept their authority as censors of the Oxford version of the poem?

❧ VIII ❧

THE TRIAL AND PUNISHMENT
OF GANELON: A CONCLUSION?

Like the Baligant episode, the trial and punishment of Ganelon represents, I believe, the poet's further response (demanded, perhaps, by the sensibility of his eleventh-century audience) to earlier, unresolved problems in his poem. Caught up in the drama of Roland's martyrdom in the first half, he had repressed certain social questions that were raised by the conflict between Roland and Ganelon. Now, in the poem's epilogue, he shows an urge to return to his material, to ponder and interpret it, to deepen it in the light of later feudal ideology.

The *Song of Roland* is as much a broad social tragedy—a tragedy of "our barons" and indeed of a whole way of life—as it is a tragedy of individual personalities. The poet leads us to an understanding of this tragedy in social terms by restaging some of the major issues in the form of a traitor's criminal trial. By doing so he translates the significance of the disaster at Ronceval into the publicly intelligible language of judicial process. The poet's consciousness of the burden of history comes close to the surface of his narrative, and with this consciousness comes the poet's role as prophet (within a feudal framework) of social reform.

How to tame the barons? Where does power reside? Where is loyalty due?[1] These questions may well have preoccupied epic narrative from Carolingian times, but they took on burning relevance for the French nobility of the late eleventh century. By this time the Capetian kings had begun to exploit the relationship between lord and vassal as a means of drawing the nobility into a more stable, centralized power structure.[2] As a genre, interestingly, the *chanson de geste* appears to have been traditionally allied with the interests of the vassal, rather than the lord, until this time.[3] In many of those epics that derive from the long oral tradition, the offender in the conflict is frequently the lord, not the vassal, and the vassal must revolt against his lord in order to restore justice and order. Yet, in these poems as *we* know them, the epic struggle that ensues never leads to any real victory; instead, the wars between vassal and lord are generally neutralized or aborted by some other narrative device, such as a reconciliation, a divine intervention, or a retraction. Quite possibly, such contradictory conclusions are the result of manipulations by later poets who reflect a reversal of social outlook: as the lord's interests were taken to heart, the literary wars against him were made to fizzle out. In another group of *chansons de geste* that were freshly composed (and not simply retold) in the twelfth century, the narrative structure is different: in these poems, the conflict is motivated by a traitor (commonly a descendant of Ganelon) who denounces a good, loyal vassal before his lord. A struggle ensues and leads ultimately to a judicial victory by the loyal vassal over the disloyal one. The apparent evolution in narrative structure of the *chanson de geste* testifies, critics believe, to this shift in political outlook. The epilogue of the *Song of Roland* reflects the same trend in late eleventh- and twelfth-century political attitudes: Ganelon must be punished for compromising the interests of Charlemagne, his lord and sovereign.

The trial and punishment of Ganelon take place at Charlemagne's administrative seat in Aachen (Aix), far from the mountains and plains of Spain. The episode is not only spatially and temporally detached from the rest of the action in the poem, but narratively, as well; for the poet formally announces that a new episode is to follow: "Now begins the trial of Ganelon" (CCLXVII). The dislocation of the trial from the narrative body of the *Song of Roland* has encouraged some critics to suspect that this episode is a late interpolation into the story, though not so late as the Baligant episode. Whether or not the trial and punishment of Ganelon figured in the earliest versions of Roland's legend, the poet who composed these episodes remains close to the spirit of revenge which propels so many of the major episodes in the poem:

> The cry of vengeance is heard at every critical moment, and the theme of revenge shapes the plot. It is Ganelon's promise of revenge on Roland that sets the whole story going (XX). The rest is guided by Charles's quest for revenge on the pagans and on Ganelon: thus when the first battle begins, "The emperor will take complete revenge" (XC); Turpin resolves the climactic quarrel between Oliver and Roland by appeal to the Emperor's revenge: "Let the king come so that he may venge us" (CXXXII); Naimon calls Charles to battle, "Venge this grievance!"

(CLXXVIII); Baligant's host must pay dearly for Roland's death (CCXVI); Charles prays to God, "May I revenge my nephew Roland" (CCXXVI); and exhorts his men, "Venge your sons, your brothers, and your heirs" (CCXLVI). Satisfaction comes at last with the execution of Ganelon, "When the emperor has taken vengeance" (CCXC).[4]

The charge brought against Ganelon is that he has provoked the personal loss to Charlemagne, his lord and sovereign, of twenty thousand Frenchmen, among whom were Roland, Oliver, and the twelve peers. The poet holds this an act of treason, and in the perspective of feudal ideology, treason was a crime of powerful moral dimensions.[5] Satan, who broke the bond of fidelity to God, is the archetypal traitor, whose crime of treason subsumes all others. Grouped in the ranks of Satan's vassals are all who are not Christian, including the Jews as murderers of Christ, the persecutors of the early Christians (such as Nero), the pagan deities, and of course, the Saracens. Beside these stand Christian traitors to vassalage such as Ganelon and his poetic successors. Ganelon's collusion with the Saracens and his treachery against Charlemagne are one and the same crime, and a crime against God. Thus, when Ganelon proposes Roland as the leader of the rearguard, Charlemagne cries out helplessly in the pain of foreknowledge, "You are a living devil!" (LVIII); and when Charlemagne charges Ganelon with treason, he lends a Biblical twist to his indictment by tacitly comparing Ganelon to Judas for having betrayed the twelve peers for money (CCLXXII). As a crime against God, Ganelon's punishment is both necessary and inevitable.

In Ganelon's case, the specific issue to be decided is whether he was justified in satisfying his honor while compromising, at the same time, the interests of his lord Charlemagne. Bristling with autistic pride, which some critics attribute to an archaic Germanic code of individualism and clannishness, Ganelon replies to Charlemagne's accusations by saying that he acted solely for personal revenge on Roland:

> Lords, I was in the emperor's army.
> I served him out of love and loyalty.
> Roland, his nephew, despised me with hate,
> And condemned me to agony and death.
> I was the messenger to King Marsile,
> But by my skill I survived the mission.
> I challenged warlike Roland, and Oliver,
> And all of their companions; Charlemagne

> Heard it; so did all his noble barons.
> I venged myself, but this was not treason. (CCLXXIII)

Ganelon's account of his actions is factually correct, but he is invoking in his own defense the sanction of an old Germanic custom (*Fehderecht*), whereby retaliation for a crime against an individual remained the responsibility of the private individual and his family. Because his challenge was public and was heard by all, Ganelon insists, he did not commit treason. Interestingly, Ganelon's defense includes what amounts to a countercharge of treason against Roland, for in the medieval mind the need for revenge (which Ganelon cites) was explicitly associated with provocation by treason.[6]

Ultimately, however, the defense of Ganelon's cause will not rest on logic but on brute force: this is the heyday of the champion rather than the lawyer. One of Ganelon's relatives, named Pinabel, readily undertakes Ganelon's defense. Pinabel is a man of formidable strength and skill, to judge by this chilly understatement of his power:

> He is large and strong and bold and quick;
> Whomever he strikes has no time left to live. (CCLXXVIII)

The spectacle of Pinabel rising in Ganelon's defense so intimidates Charlemagne's barons that they hush their voices in fear and agree to urge that Charlemagne drop the whole indictment:

> Bavarians and Saxons go to council,
> And Poitevins and Normands and the French.
> Numerous Germans and Tiedois too were there.
> Those from Auvergne were noblest of them all.
> Because of Pinabel they speak in whispers.
> One says to the other, "Let's stay where we are.
> Let us forget the trial and ask the king
> That Ganelon be acquitted this one time,
> And that Ganelon serve him in love and good faith.
> Roland is dead, and we'll see him no more.
> Gold or riches will never bring him back.
> Only a mighty fool would fight. . . ." (CCLXXV)

When Charlemagne hears the barons' recommendation, he is enraged by their cowardice and exclaims, "You are traitors!" He feels betrayed, no doubt, because his barons are shirking their responsibility of delivering justice, a duty explicitly called for by the bond between vassal and lord. One would have expected Charlemagne's barons to defend

underlying the surface of events. Without trying to vindicate Roland, Thierry claims that Ganelon was wrong to exact revenge on Roland because Roland at the time was in the emperor's service: Roland was not just Roland, in other words, but a representative of Charles; thus, Ganelon's pact of retaliation constituted treason. In Thierry's words,

> "Though Roland did injury to Ganelon,
> His service to you was his protection.
> Ganelon is a traitor for betraying him:
> Ganelon betrayed you in betraying him.
> He perjured himself and caused you damage.
> For this I judge that he die by hanging." (CCLXXVII)

One suspects, in instances like this, that the premises of the *Song of Roland* are changing as the poem progresses. Roland was allowed to die secure in his honor, to be sure, yet retrospectively the barons now seem to acknowledge that Roland bears considerable personal blame for initiating the catastrophe at Ronceval by provoking Ganelon. In any case, Thierry, the man who finally exacts vengeance on Ganelon and who succeeds Roland as Charlemagne's champion, is a far cry from the quick and unreflective hero that Roland was. True, a hundred thousand knights "weep in pity for Thierry for Roland's sake," yet we can only feel that Roland would be out of place in Thierry's brave new world. Roland is dead, and so are the twelve peers. Faceless as he is, Thierry is what some critics have called the "new man," a perfect spokesman for the establishment.

The procedure by which Ganelon is actually convicted takes the form of a judicial duel.[7] A legacy of ancient Germanic and Carolingian custom, the judicial duel remained an instrument of feudal law beyond the twelfth century. The duel is related to the "ordeal" (cognate with the German, *Urteil*), where an accused man would be ordered to grasp a red-hot iron with his hands; if he emerged unscarred, he was innocent. (A literary example of such justice may be found in the tale of *Tristan and Isolde*.) Both the judicial duel and the ordeal were based on a belief that God's will is immanent in terrestrial affairs, and that God, who is the very principle of justice, will intervene in the operations of mankind whenever the cause of justice is in jeopardy. In a large sense, the whole *Song of Roland* may be conceived as a judicial duel between the true and false gods, enacted by their respective champions on earth.

Generally, the judici
where evidence was insu
In Ganelon's case, how
Ganelon's actions: the n
ambiguous to all. The p
substance of the tragedy
ciety but also to remove
against a powerful vassa
and to ratify such a judgn

Although the Christiar
own justice, nevertheless
(CCLXXX) before the du
Pinabel is the first to kno
casion to propose a deal
cussion and rushes back ir
bel, and now *he* is in a
suddenly arrested, and fc
clarity an encounter of per
"new man" has the upper
precedented in this poem,
mires his enemy and exhorts

> Says Thierry, "Pin
> You are very great
> Your peers respect y
> Give up this battle;
> I will have you reco
> Justice will be done
> Such that men will s

It almost seems as though h
can a new, benevolent socia
old guard? Can the ethic of r
self-destruction, be abrogated
miraculous spirit of reconcilia
Can the flow of human blood
love? These are questions tha
ask and answer for itself. Unf
poet, who must formulate such
idiom of the poem and perhap

the poet himself
justified or not,
remains true to
brook no compr
returns, at the e
oped potential) t
formulas that su
absolute commitr

> Pinabe
> I shall
> And n
> It is b
> With
> Their
> Sparks
> Nothi
> Unles

When at last P
divine justice, t

> It is ver
> And his

Accordingly, al
that "tree of cu
as he is quarte
form of punish
of revenge, ho
the poet breal
that traitors m
haps detect a n
Once the m
ample earned
ignominy. Da
was simply

Ganelon in order to preserve their honor and political autonomy from Charlemagne, but such is not their motive. They act not out of self-respect but because they are afraid. Is it not possible that the poet is deliberately undermining the cause of political autonomy here by making its proponents seem sleazy and dissolute instead of heroic?

At the moment when justice and authority and leadership seem to have perished from the face of the earth, a dissenting vassal appears before Charlemagne to take up his cause:

> When Charlemagne sees that all have failed him,
> He lowers his face and his body slumps.
> He cries out in pain because of his grief.
> A knight appears before him named Thierry,
> Geoffrey's brother, an Angevine duke. (CCLXXVII)

The poet was generous with Pinabel, Ganelon's champion: well built, handsome, respected by his peers, and forceful of speech, he is a typical heroic warrior. Thierry, by contrast, is a man of modest and even unpromising proportions; courageous, to be sure, but essentially faceless. Unlike Pinabel, Thierry is a subtle man, and his subtlety translates itself into a portrait fraught with qualifications and innuendoes:

> His body was thin, as if underfed;
> His hair was black, his skin was almost brown.
> He was not large; but then, he was not small. (CCLXXVII)

The contrast between Pinabel and Thierry, between hero and anti-hero, is vividly conceived and serves several purposes. Dramatically, it heightens our suspense; how can justice possibly win out against such odds? Politically, the contrast invites us to re-evaluate the role of the uncomplicated, old-style warrior in society in the light of a less glorious, less attractive man who stands for social order and whose courage takes the paradoxical form of selfless devotion to the interests of his lord. Ethically, the presence of Thierry disputes the fundamental assumption that "might is right," which is implicit in the heroic spirit. Thierry even redefines the goals of dynastic pride and chivalric honor by saying to Charlemagne, "By my ancestors I must uphold your plea" (CCLXXVII).

Thierry is lucid in his formulation of the charges against Ganelon. He recognizes, first of all, what is obvious, that Roland injured Ganelon. Like Oliver, Thierry is both able and willing to consider realities underlying the surface of events. Without trying to vindicate Roland, Thierry claims that Ganelon was wrong to exact revenge on Roland because Roland at the time was in the emperor's service: Roland was not just Roland, in other words, but a representative of Charles; thus, Ganelon's pact of retaliation constituted treason. In Thierry's words,

> "Though Roland did injury to Ganelon,
> His service to you was his protection.
> Ganelon is a traitor for betraying him:
> Ganelon betrayed you in betraying him.
> He perjured himself and caused you damage.
> For this I judge that he die by hanging." (CCLXXVII)

One suspects, in instances like this, that the premises of the *Song of Roland* are changing as the poem progresses. Roland was allowed to die secure in his honor, to be sure, yet retrospectively the barons now seem to acknowledge that Roland bears considerable personal blame for initiating the catastrophe at Ronceval by provoking Ganelon. In any case, Thierry, the man who finally exacts vengeance on Ganelon and who succeeds Roland as Charlemagne's champion, is a far cry from the quick and unreflective hero that Roland was. True, a hundred thousand knights "weep in pity for Thierry for Roland's sake," yet we can only feel that Roland would be out of place in Thierry's brave new world. Roland is dead, and so are the twelve peers. Faceless as he is, Thierry is what some critics have called the "new man," a perfect spokesman for the establishment.

The procedure by which Ganelon is actually convicted takes the form of a judicial duel.[7] A legacy of ancient Germanic and Carolingian custom, the judicial duel remained an instrument of feudal law beyond the twelfth century. The duel is related to the "ordeal" (cognate with the German, *Urteil*), where an accused man would be ordered to grasp a red-hot iron with his hands; if he emerged unscarred, he was innocent. (A literary example of such justice may be found in the tale of *Tristan and Isolde*.) Both the judicial duel and the ordeal were based on a belief that God's will is immanent in terrestrial affairs, and that God, who is the very principle of justice, will intervene in the operations of mankind whenever the cause of justice is in jeopardy. In a large sense, the whole *Song of Roland* may be conceived as a judicial duel between the true and false gods, enacted by their respective champions on earth.

Generally, the judicial duel was reserved for extraordinary cases where evidence was insufficient to permit a judgment on other grounds. In Ganelon's case, however, there is no lack of "evidence" regarding Ganelon's actions: the nature of both the deed and the motive is unambiguous to all. The poet seems to wish not only to dramatize the substance of the tragedy of personalities in the judicial forms of society but also to remove the burden of rendering a painful judgment against a powerful vassal from the confused sphere of mortal affairs and to ratify such a judgment against Ganelon with the will of God.

Although the Christian God allows men to be the agents of their own justice, nevertheless "God knows very well what the end will be" (CCLXXX) before the duel between Thierry and Pinabel takes place. Pinabel is the first to knock down his adversary, and he seizes the occasion to propose a deal to acquit Ganelon. Thierry rejects all discussion and rushes back into action. Next, Thierry knocks down Pinabel, and now *he* is in a position to make proposals. The action is suddenly arrested, and for an instant we witness with emblematic clarity an encounter of perspectives between the old and the new. The "new man" has the upper hand. In a flow of surprising charity, unprecedented in this poem, a victorious warrior openly loves and admires his enemy and exhorts him to put aside his weapons:

> Says Thierry, "Pinabel, you are very brave;
> You are very great and strong; your body is well built;
> Your peers respect you as a noble vassal.
> Give up this battle; put fighting aside.
> I will have you reconciled with Charles.
> Justice will be done on Ganelon,
> Such that men will speak of it forever." (CCLXXXIV)

It almost seems as though history itself were hanging in the balance: can a new, benevolent social order encompass the fierce glory of the old guard? Can the ethic of revenge, founded on destruction and even self-destruction, be abrogated, as it was at the end of the *Odyssey*, by a miraculous spirit of reconciliation in the higher order of a just peace? Can the flow of human blood be stanched by an outpouring of human love? These are questions that every society, including our own, must ask and answer for itself. Unfortunately, *we* are the ones, and not the poet, who must formulate such questions here, for they lie beyond the idiom of the poem and perhaps even beyond the conceptual powers of the poet himself. The answer to these questions, whether they are justified or not, is clear: here as everywhere in the poem, the hero remains true to his identity. Pinabel's honor (as he conceives it) can brook no compromise. Thus, there can be no clemency; and the poet returns, at the end of this *laisse* (so pregnant with fresh but undeveloped potential) to the most proven formulas of the epic poet's trade, formulas that summarize with unwelcome finality the heroic warrior's absolute commitment to destruction:

> Pinabel says, "May it not please God!
> I shall uphold the cause of any kinsman,
> And not default for any mortal man.
> It is better to die than feel reproach."
> With their swords they now begin to strike
> Their helmets made of studded gold and gems.
> Sparks now brightly fly into the air.
> Nothing, now, can separate these men:
> Unless one dies, this battle cannot end. (CCLXXXIV)

When at last Pinabel's brain is cleft, as it must be, by the sword of divine justice, the French barons all cry out,

> "God has shown his power!
> It is very right that Ganelon be hanged,
> And his kinsmen too, who pleaded for him." (CCLXXXVII)

Accordingly, all thirty of Ganelon's relatives are summarily hanged on that "tree of cursed wood." Ganelon himself suffers "marvelous pain" as he is quartered by four horses: such seems to be the traditional form of punishment for treason against one's sovereign.[8] The climate of revenge, however, proffers no relief. On the contrary, three times the poet breaks out of his narrative voice to admonish us directly that traitors must be punished thus. In such urgency may we not perhaps detect a new longing for public order?

Once the most famous traitor of medieval poetry was dead, his example earned for him in the medieval mind a place unmatched for ignominy. Dante put him in the ninth circle of hell; for Chaucer he was simply

> . . . the false Genelloun,
> He that purchased the treasoun
> Of Rowland and of Olyver.[9]

With Ganelon dead there is justice, but no joy. If we think back to the first half of the poem, where knights killed and were killed for their lord and where death seemed almost like an excess of life, we now sense that a whole mode of life, a whole system of values, has become exhausted. Evil has been destroyed, to be sure, and revenge is complete: yet, the ethic of revenge has left the world bitter and empty. Along with Roland and the twelve peers and the twenty thousand knights of the rearguard, a heroic order has perished. Even their glory has perished, in a sense, because the men who remain can remember it but cannot inherit it. In short, of all the stuff that epics are made of, nothing remains. There is only Charlemagne, the last survivor of a heroic age, but a hero grown old. To be killed in a heroic poem is not to die but to complete all one has lived for; thus, for Roland, death was an elevation, an apotheosis, anything but the end of life. To be deprived of action and yet to live on in a heroic poem, however, is nothing less than death-in-life, for the true hero lives by action. It is a paradox, perhaps, that the experience of loss and annihilation, which we commonly associate with death, should be conveyed to us by a figure who can*not* die. We should understand, though, that Charlemagne has come to love others more than himself, and by virtue of this love has lost far more life than he could lose by dying himself.

The figure of the old hero is common enough in epic poetry—men such as Nestor, Priam, Romulus, Beowulf, and Calidore come immediately to mind. In most epics that I know of, however, the waning of a life is a theme woven into a broader social fabric which contains, as well, a world that is still vigorous and young. In this poem, the supreme old age of Charlemagne has become the central fact of the world; and his alienation from the time of his own Roland-like youth may be taken as a metaphor, perhaps, for the poet's (and his audience's) sense of remoteness from that age in the tenth century when heroic glory was a possible and honorable goal in life, that violent age where lay the true roots of French oral epic poetry.

One might have expected that Ganelon's execution would offer an architecturally neat conclusion to the *Song of Roland*: after all, vengeance is complete and social order, however tenuous, is restored. The tendency of oral epic narrative, however, is to be *in*conclusive, to be open-ended, and to lead to new beginnings. As an entity, the oral poem is ephemeral. Such was the case with the *Iliad,* which ended with an implied resumption of the Trojan War, and such now is the case with the *Song of Roland*. Superficially, at least, the narrative of the *Roland* points to a new departure. In my opinion, however, the two concluding *laisses* of the *Song of Roland* furnish, in their own terse way, a remarkable surprise, difficult to assess and easy, perhaps, to overinterpret. I quote the first *laisse:*

> When the emperor's revenge was finished,
> He summoned together bishops from France,
> Those of Bavaria and Germany:
> "In my house I hold a noble prisoner.
> She has heard so many sermons and parables
> That she wishes to believe in God and asks
> To be converted to Christianity.
> Baptize her, so that God may have her soul."
> They reply, "Let it be done, with sponsors!" . . .
> In the waters of Aix they baptized her
> The Queen of Spain, and named her Julianne.
> She came to Christ through knowledge of the truth.

It might be argued that this is just one more formulaic *laisse,* whose main purpose is to illustrate the magnanimity of a conquering Christian ruler—certainly, Charlemagne was celebrated in legend as having made innumerable conversions to the Christian faith. It might be argued, as well, that because the poem's ending, as it now stands, points to new narrative episodes, this *laisse* is of little consequence to the poem as a whole. My own belief, however, is that this *laisse* and the last *laisse* in the poem were conceived (however formulaically) as a thematic conclusion to the poem and that they are poignant and rich with meaning if one is willing to grant, as I am, that the *Song of Roland* is governed, however open-ended it may be, by a sense of artistic design.

Charlemagne's noble prisoner is Bramimonde, who has loved Marsile, the very man who caused the death of Roland. Except for the fact that she is a woman (which is not apparently a significant fact in this precourtly poem), Charlemagne has more reason to despise her than anyone else who remains alive in the world. At the same time, she is the only person in the *Song of Roland* who has experienced a personal tragedy equivalent to Charlemagne's own. She has lost her husband, her son, and all her people—in short, everyone on earth whom she has loved. As Achilles, near the end of the *Iliad,* was drawn to Priam, the father of his worst enemy, so Charlemagne is perhaps drawn to his enemy precisely because she is the only figure in the poem who has suffered in life as much as he. Does the poet not show by example that in a man who has truly suffered, the impulse to love another human being and to share his agony is more fundamental than any other, including the impulse to hate an enemy? True charity is frequently paradoxical in the object it selects; instead of punishing Bramimonde, therefore, Charlemagne gives her the best that a medieval Christian could give to another human being: Christ himself. Following so closely after an episode of grim vindictiveness, this outpouring of charity in Charlemagne alleviates, to some extent, the poem's bitterness by causing in us, as well, an instantaneous outpouring, an opening of the heart in sympathy. Until the combat between Thierry and Pinabel, throughout this poem the poet has stressed Christianity as a religion of revenge, triumph, and salvation: now, perhaps intuitively, the poet stresses Christianity as a religion of compassion for others and of charity which takes on full meaning in a context of human suffering on earth. One thinks of the difference between early medieval representations of Christ on the cross—rigid, composed, angular, regal even in pain—and later medieval crucifixes, where Christ manifestly suffers, displays his wounds, and evokes pity.

The opening lines of the final *laisse* summarize and reinforce the momentary thaw in the climate of revenge caused by the release of compassion, but the lines that follow suggest yet another dimension in the poet's final outlook:

> When the emperor has done his justice,
> And when he had relieved his mighty wrath,
> He brought the Christian faith to Bramimonde.
> The day passed by, and the night brought darkness.
> The king went to bed in his vaulted chamber.
> Saint Gabriel came from God to tell him:
> "Charles, summon the armies of your empire!
> By force you will go to the land of Bire,
> You will aid King Vivian in Imphe,
> At the walls where the pagans have set siege.
> Christians call for you and cry for aid."
> The emperor does not wish to set forth:
> "Lord," says the king, "such anguish in my life!"
> His eyes weep, he pulls on his white beard.
> Here ends the *geste* that Turold has compiled. (CCXCI)

We will notice, first of all, that the direction of the narrative in the final *laisse* is away from the complexities of the exterior, social world and toward the privacy of Charlemagne as an individual. We observed a similar direction in the movement of the poem's first half, which gradually carried us away from the mayhem of battle to a staged and climatic soliloquy by an isolated hero. In both halves of the *Song of Roland,* then, we detect an attraction in the poet's mind toward the realm of individual, subjective experience—this in spite of the fundamentally public nature of his formulaic idiom. One wonders if, by dramatically isolating Charlemagne, the poet is not anticipating that transition from the public world of epic to the intimacy of romance which is about to occur in French narrative poetry.

As if better to accommodate Charlemagne's final moment of solitariness, the setting of the poem moves indoors (except for Charlemagne's dreams, the *Roland* is an *out*door poem) to the emperor's bedchamber. For an instant we are situated in a space that is dislocated from the warrior's world, a place where reflection and contemplation are more in order than deeds. Accordingly, Charlemagne's personality takes on new complexity: now he is at odds with the role that destiny has thrust upon him.[10] When Roland died, we may recall, we found no trace of disillusionment, no sense that his travail on earth had led him to any new understanding about life that he did not possess at the poem's outset. Roland's dying moments were the uncomplicated apogee of a heroic career, and Roland's triumphant attitude in death merely confirmed his glory as a hero. Such is not the case with Charlemagne. A Roland grown old, Charlemagne has outlived the hero's thirst for martial glory. The hero's honor means little to him. More than any other character in the poem, Charlemagne perceives the consequences of the warfaring life for what they are, and his reaction is despair. Charlemagne feels only inconsolable loss because all his best men have destroyed themselves, and now he must depart anew. Nothing seems to have been gained after so much struggling, unless it is the revelation of another person's suffering.

Charlemagne does not die. Sick with life ("Lord, such anguish in my life!"), Charlemagne (unlike Beowulf) cannot die until the genre dies. It would not have occurred to the poet to dispatch his hero with a literary *coup de grace* in order to preserve his dignity, as Cervantes did with Don Quixote. Although we sense exhaustion in both hero and poem, the poet nevertheless maintains the conventional cast of his work until the very last lines. Charlemagne is his most characteristic and formulaic self in the final *laisse* as he weeps from his eyes and pulls on his white beard. He has not changed since he entered the poem, but what earlier were hyperboles of grief, which almost seemed unwarranted, have become understatement in the total desolation of the emperor's world. The poet's formulaic language can barely sustain, now, the tragic burden of his conclusion and seems ready to explode with emotion. Charlemagne has fulfilled the potential of his own formulas, and both he and the poet are on the verge, perhaps, of reaching out for new values in life. But these cannot be explored in the idiom of the *Song of Roland*. Thus, the poet's style and his material remain intact until the poem's very end. But *barely* intact: the city of Imphe in the land of Bire, both imaginary, seem infinitely far compared with Spain, at least as we see them through the eyes of a two-hundred-year-old warrior. Will Charlemagne resist the mission that his Lord and maker has given him? The question does not arise in the poem, yet it is clear to us that in Charlemagne's tragic vision, the task of life has become far more bitter than the prospect of death. This is the moment when men of the ordinary world would surely yield, yet this is precisely the moment when the epic hero defines himself and reveals, thereby, the distance between his world and our own; of *course* Charlemagne will depart for Imphe in the land of Bire. What is possible will win out over what is probable, and epic art will win out over reality, for this poem—like all epic poems—is an expression of faith (not just Christian faith) in the superbly beautiful and human paradox that man is capable of perceiving the futility of this world and still of struggling for an ideal in life.

To judge by the ending of this poem, in the eleventh century it was possible and perhaps necessary to believe in the myth of Charlemagne, and we may say that a poetic style has stood the test of its own time. But the *Song of Roland* is more than a masterpiece of feudal culture. The explicit terms of failure and achievement in life may change with the centuries, yet certain goals remain permanent in man's aspirations. The reader who looks beneath what is distinctly feudal or medieval—or even Christian—about the *Song of Roland* will find in it those images of loyalty, courage, and dignity in suffering which are the constant concerns of all epic and which have rightfully earned for this poem a privileged place in Western narrative tradition.

CHRONOLOGY

476	The definitive collapse of the Roman Empire.
570	The birth of Mohammed.
633	Beginning of the Arab conquest: Syria, Egypt, Persia.
696–708	The conquest of Africa by the Arabs.
711	The Arabs take Spain; the Visigothic monarchy collapses.
732	Charles Martel defeats the Arabs at Poitiers.
741	Charles Martel dies.
751	The beginning of the Carolingian dynasty: Pépin le Bref is annointed by Saint Boniface.
754	Alliance between the Papacy and the Carolingian monarchy.
768	The ascendancy of Charlemagne: the beginning of a reign oriented toward extending the Frankish kingdom and, simultaneously, the expansion of the Christian Empire.
771	Charlemagne is the sole ruler of the Franks.
778	Charlemagne, blessed by Pope Hadrian, undertakes a personal campaign against Saragossa: Roland dies, August 15, as Charlemagne's rearguard is attacked by Basques or by Arabs in league with Basques.
800	Charlemagne is crowned emperor on Christmas Day at Rome by Pope Leo III.
814	Charlemagne dies and is succeeded by Louis le Pieux.
829–30	First mention in official chronicles of Charlemagne's defeat at Ronceval. Einhard publishes his *Life of Charlemagne*.
843	Division of the Carolingian Empire among Lothaire, Louis, and Charles.
847	The Arabs sack Rome.
880–87	The former Carolingian Empire is briefly reconstituted but finally disintegrates into multiple kingships.
936	Otto I consecrated at Aachen (Aix).
987	Hugh Capet takes power in France.

1000	Otto III opens Charlemagne's tomb in Aachen.
1054	Schism between East and West.
1066	The Norman conquest of England under William the Conqueror.
1095	The Council of Clermont: Pope Urban II preaches the First Crusade.
1095–1100 (?)	The Oxford version of the *Song of Roland* is composed.
1147	The Second Crusade departs under Louis VII.
1165	Frederic I attempts to have Charlemagne canonized by the anti-pope.

APPENDIX II

THE HISTORICAL EVENT

What is the historical basis underlying the tale of Roland and the drama at Ronceval? Unfortunately for us, this whole historical episode occurred at a time when contemporary documents were scanty, irregular, and even deceitful. More than a few scholars have devoted their careers to this single problem, excavating the earth, opening graves, hunting among the archives of Europe, deciphering Arab chronicles, and extrapolating theories from unreliable monastic chronicles. They have emerged with an inconclusive, disputed sketch of the historical event, whose outlines are as follows.

Exactly three centuries after the definitive collapse of Rome, which we conventionally place in A.D. 476, civil war was rampant among the Moselm governors of Spain. The Omayyad Abd Al Rahman of Cordova had declared himself independent of the Abbasid Caliphs, and struggles of power had ensued. A rebellion within a rebellion complicated the situation when Al Arabi, governor of Barcelona, and Ansari, governor of Saragossa, allied themselves against Al Rahman at a time when the latter was already at war with the Abbasids. Al Rahman still managed to dispatch a general to break the insurgent governors, but this general was defeated and taken hostage in A.D. 777.

Al Arabi decided that he should fortify his independence from Cordova by soliciting the aid of Charlemagne, then king of the Franks. So he journeyed to Charlemagne, who at that moment had just finished subjecting the Saxons. Charlemagne was interested by Al Arabi's proposal that he come to Spain and fight against Al Rahman. Al Arabi proposed to submit to Charlemagne's rule in exchange for support, and Charlemagne was apparently enthusiastic at the prospect of extending his territory across the Pyrenees.

By the spring of the following year (A.D. 778) he was at Poitiers, where he joined with forces from Neustria and Aquitania whom he personally led over the Pyrenees into Spain. Crossing through Navarre (taking Pamplona without violence on the way), Charlemagne went to Saragossa. There he met a column of his own forces which had come from the eastern sector of his realm (Austrasia, Bavaria, Lombardy, Provence) by way of Barcelona; Al Arabi, the emir of Barcelona was with them. When Charlemagne arrived at Saragossa, however, he was greeted only by the closed walls and hostility of his former supplicant, Al Ansari, who may have feared a conspiracy against him between Charlemagne and Al Arabi. Charlemagne and his army camped beneath the walls of Saragossa for a month and a half before news that a new revolt was erupting in Saxony prompted him to hasten home. They departed with Al Arabi as hostage, but the latter's sons (according to Arab chronicles) attacked the Frankish columns and retrieved their father. This first engagement occurred between the river Ebro and Pamplona. Charlemagne continued on his journey homeward, destroying Pamplona for reasons of security on the way. However, while they were crossing the Pyrenees they were assaulted a second time, this time by a band of Basques (perhaps in league with some Moslems) who executed a disastrously effective ambush in the narrows of the mountain pass. A number of Charlemagne's best leaders died in the attack, which occurred on August 15, 778.

The Basque ambush put Charlemagne's political destiny into jeopardy for a time, especially because the wildly insurgent Saxons constituted a real threat to his power. Curiously enough, however, the official chronicles maintained strict silence about the whole disaster. Why? Was it to flatter the king, or to intimidate his contemporaries with the illusion of a perfect political and military record? We do not really know. We know only that the truth was systematically camouflaged by chroniclers until well after the emperor's death. Only around 830 did mention of the disaster at Ronceval first creep into the official documents. The first break in this confusing silence occurred in the so-called *Royal Annals Until 829*, which were revised decades after the event itself. Even then, the entry concerning the event is scant.[1] The first account that pretends to show anything but the most cursory concern for what happened is Einhard's (written also as "Eginhard") statement in his panegyrical biography of Charlemagne:

> In the midst of this vigorous and almost uninterrupted struggle with the Saxons, he covered the frontier by garrisons at the proper points, and marched over the Pyrenees to Spain at the head of all the forces which he could muster. All the towns and castles that he attacked surrendered, and up to the time of his homeward march he sustained no loss whatever; but on his return through the Pyrenees he had cause to rue the treachery

of the Gascons. That region is well adapted for ambuscades by reason of the thick forests that cover it; and as the army advanced in the long line of march necessitated by the narrowness of the road, the Gascons, who lay in ambush at the top of a very high mountain, attacked the rear of the baggage train and the rear-guard in charge of it and hurled them down to the very bottom of the valley. In the struggle that ensued, they cut them off to the man; they then plundered the baggage, and dispersed with all speed in every direction under cover of approaching night. The lightness of their armor, and the nature of the battle-ground stood the Gascons in good stead on this occasion whereas the Franks fought at a disadvantage in every respect, because of the weight of their armor and because of the unevenness of the ground. Eggihard, the King's steward; Anselm, Count Palatine; and Roland (Hruodlandus), Governor of the March of Brittany, with very many others fell in this engagement. This ill turn could not be avenged for the nonce, because the enemy scattered so widely after carrying out their plan that not the least clue could be had to their whereabouts.[2]

Some scholars optimistically identify this *Hruodlandus,* a Frankish chief who perished in the incident, as the historical figure behind the epic hero of this poem. They support this contention with additional evidence, such as the appearance of the name "Rodlan" on three Carolingian coins and the knowledge that a certain *Rothlandus,* a palatine *fidelis,* served as a judge in important litigations around 772.[3]

Such is the evidence for the historicity of Roland and the drama of Ronceval. It is most meager and has often been hotly disputed. Finally, we know no more about the drama at Ronceval than we know about the Trojan War underlying Homer's story in the *Iliad.* Only the legend of Arthur is more vague.

In our uncertainty, then, we have no license to affirm that Roland ever existed; by the same token, we have no reason to deny, either, that a man named Roland died in an ambush in the Pyrenees in August 778. But we have every reason to believe that the beautiful poem that we possess in the Oxford manuscript of the *Song of Roland* was composed at the end of the eleventh century or during the first quarter of the twelfth century, at the latest. A great mystery remains to be solved, one similar to the mystery of the *Iliad*: how did the story of Ronceval, like the story of Troy, survive the so-called "silence of the centuries" and emerge as a full-blown epic three (and in the case of Homer, possibly four) hundred years later? In what form did that nucleus of truth wend its way through time to inform the first extant masterpiece of French culture? The history of this question—

familiarly known among scholars as *la question rolandienne*—is a fascinating subject, both for the perspective it offers on a century of modern scholarship and for the brilliant and intriguing answers which a whole army of perplexed critics have provided, or else failed to provide. We shall summarize this story in the following appendix.

⋖§ APPENDIX III ℥⋗

ROLAND AND THE CRITICS:

A SYNOPSIS

For all its flamboyance, the *Song of Roland* remains a poem of closely guarded secrets. Aside from the vexation of our not knowing when, where, or by whom the poem was composed, there are countless subtler questions of coherence, structure, style, and poetic intention which defy any certain answers.

Because the *Song of Roland* has strong appeal, able critics have always been drawn to it; because it is finally inscrutable, these critics have enjoyed considerable license to "discover" in the poem whatever their preconceptions about the nature of epic poetry and of medieval culture *urged* them to discover. The criticism that has accumulated around the *Song of Roland* (and other Old French epics) is therefore full of contrary interpretations, reflecting major shifts of literary theory and of attitudes toward the medieval world that have occurred since the manuscript was discovered. Whoever makes the effort to explore this criticism, not only will learn a great deal about the *Song of Roland* and about medieval culture in general, but will find that an exciting chronicle of conflicting literary theory has developed since the first ideas of the romantic movement were matched by minds of later generations, no less speculative, ingenious, or polemical than their forebears.

I include this summary of major critical theories for several reasons.[1] First, I wish to arm the reader, however lightly, with a certain amount of perspective if he reads a book about the *Song of Roland*: there are usually two (or more) sides to every critical question about the poem. Second, I wish to encourage readers to evaluate their own literary premises by encountering the meticulous arguments of others. Third, I wish to stress that a literary question is a product of its age, and that new generations of readers owe it to themselves to bring new questions to the poem. This third point is most urgent, in my opinion, because a large number of modern medievalists have allowed themselves to become trapped by great, "respectable" questions, which have lost their potential for providing truly fresh and vital readings of the poem. The *Song of Roland* deserves better.

The circumstances surrounding the discovery of the manuscript are themselves indicative of a distinct literary climate. During the decade of the 1830's, when medievalism had already become widely fashionable in France—owing partially to the influence of writers such as Chateaubriand, Madame de Staël and Victor Hugo—a young Frenchman named Francisque Michel set out for England to trace a manuscript dealing with the story of Ronceval.[2] Its existence had already been suggested to him through a casual allusion made some years earlier by an English editor of Chaucer. Some poetic versions of the legend were already known in fragments, and in July 1835, Michel was able to write from England that he had found a new one. This was the *Song of Roland* as we know it. Michel transcribed the poem and published it two years later. The manuscript—now called the "Oxford" manuscript—contained a text of 3,998 decasyllabic verses grouped in 291 assonanced *laisses*. Written in one column on a parchment of mediocre quality and small dimensions (17 × 12 cm.), the text had been bound during the thirteenth century with a Latin translation of Plato's *Timaeus* (strange bedfellows!). More than seven hundred years of obscurity, it will be noticed, separate the execution of the manuscript from its first modern printing.

The first important attempt to account for the existence of the *Song of Roland* as we know it in the Oxford version came from Gaston Paris several decades after its discovery. Paris applied to the poem the romantic ideas about collective authorship that had become standard in his time. His *Histoire poétique de Charlemagne* (1865) marks the beginning of a massive scholarly debate, which still rages. He argued that the warriors who survived the disaster at Ronceval must have returned home and expressed their grief over the event with spontaneous songs. These songs or *cantilènes* (from the Latin, *cantilena*) were lyrical, so the theory goes, rather than narrative, and were passed from generation to generation from the eighth century to the tenth. With time, the memory of the event faded, and these lyrical songs were expanded with narrative material both new and old until they finally reached their form as mature epic poems.[3] At the roots of this theory lie two important early romantic assumptions: first, poetry and history are originally inseparable; second, a poetic movement grows "organically," that is, it germinates, matures, and declines like a living organism.

Gaston Paris is the first spokesman among critics of the *Song of Roland* for the so-called "traditionalist" view, which holds that the *chanson de geste* is an outgrowth of popular genius, of that collective, national soul which survived the darkness of the centuries by nurturing its historical memories through poetic songs. Skepticism at Paris's theory of origins was immediate. An Italian critic named Pio Rajna, for example, argued that the meaning of the word *cantilène* is not at all clear and may always have meant *chanson de geste* (and not song), as it did later in chronicles of the twelfth century.[4] Thus, in deriving from *cantilènes, chansons de geste* may have derived from *chansons de geste* and not from short, lyrical "songs." Rajna argues, then, for an unbroken epic tradition ever since the eighth century, but his premises remain otherwise basically in harmony with standard romantic doctrines of literary genesis.

Like any great movement, romanticism was vast enough to contain contradictions. Under the spell of German idealism, certain theorists were repulsed by the idea of collective authorship and saw the epic poem as a sublime creation *ex nihilo* of the individual imagination, the expression of a unique, creative human spirit.[5] This view, in which the *Song of Roland* became the least "popular" of poems, was put forward by Joseph Bédier.[6] He attacked the evidence for that core of historicity that was supposedly intact in *Roland* and emphasized all that is *anti*-historical in the poem—and there is a great deal —arguing instead for a spontaneous literary creation by a single intelligence. Where "traditionalists" sought contradictions in the tale that they could attribute to the imperfect assimilation of material contributed by different epochs, Bédier sought unity, coherence, and internal logic, which might prove that the poem was of single authorship. He believed that the great themes of the *Song of Roland* emerged only during the eleventh century, and not before: Charlemagne against the pagans, Roland the Christian martyr, Turpin the warrior-prelate, "sweet France"—for Bédier all of these themes reflect the later age of the crusades against Spain and the Holy Land.

It is interesting to note that trends in nineteenth-century nationalism found expression even in the seemingly esoteric theories of epic origins. The early French romantics had looked to Germany and the northern European countries as a main cultural force, and the traditionalists had wanted to find the source for *chanson de geste* in Carolingian and Merovingian times—hence, to make them Germanic in origin. But Joseph Bédier, writing at the turn of the last century when the vogue of Teutonism in France had lost its appeal (partially because of the Franco-Prussian war of 1870), was anxious to reclaim French culture from the taint of Germanism; hence, the *Song of Roland* became, in his eyes, a later work of purely French inspiration, the art of a *Franc de France*.[7]

When he had destroyed the principal theories of traditionalism about collective authorship of the *Roland*, Bédier was at last obliged to provide a theory of his own. Accordingly, he hypothesized that during the time preceding the creation of French epic poetry, there had existed local legends—insignificant, monkish creations—attached to various sites along the pilgrim routes of France; these legends had lain inert until that *minute sacrée* when some poet of genius wandering along these same routes discovered the legendary material and converted it spontaneously into French epic poetry. Bédier believed that this "sacred minute" transpired sometime between 1098 and 1100.[8] He ends one summary of his theory with an oft-quoted, sonorous and semiliturgical pronouncement: "Before the *chansons de geste*, the local legend, the legend of the Church; in the beginning was the route, strewn with sanctuaries."[9]

Bédier completed the expression of his theories just before World War I, and they caused a variety of reactions among critics. Some reversed his theories and argued for the pre-existence of a poetic tradition.[10] Others carried the doctrines of the creative poetical imagination even further, dispensing altogether with legend and sanctuary to assert the primacy of the poem itself: first came the poem and *then* the legend.[11] Critics have labeled those theories that argue for a single author "individualist," and the division between the traditionalists and the individualists closely reflects a similar division between the so-called "separatists" and "unitarians" of Homeric scholarship who argue, respectively, for and against the notion of multiple authorship in Homer's epics.

One branch of individualist critics deserves mention in passing, though it has made no significant contribution to our understanding of French epics (except, perhaps, by default): this is the small number of critics who believe that the French vernacular epic derives from classical sources, principally the *Aeneid* and Lucan's *Pharsalia*.[12] It may quite simply be said, however, that no critic has found a single detail in the *Song of Roland* to substantiate the idea of any direct influence of either classical or medieval Latin epic on this vernacular poem. There is, admittedly, an odd verse in *Roland* (2,626) where the poet asserts that Baligant "lived longer than Virgil and Homer," but nothing warrants our believing that the poet identifies these names with the art of poetry rather than senility.

Bédier was a sensitive and gifted reader of poetry, and his irreversible achievement was to restore artistic dignity to the Oxford version of the *Roland*. However, as scholars labored over the question of origins, the *question rolandienne*, more and more evidence turned up which lent weight to the ideas of traditionalism. Of particular importance was our realization that the *Song of Roland* derives to a great extent from a popular, oral narrative tradition. Investigation of oral technique has followed the initiative of Homeric scholars, who have studied the properties of formulaic composition among bards in Yugoslavia still capable of reciting long, improvised narrative poems from memory. The discovery that the *Roland* has roots in an oral tradition does not preclude the possibility that a single, literate poet wrote the poem, but it does allow some certainty that there was a long narrative background to both the poem's epic material and its epic idiom. Research from other quarters reinforces such a belief. René Louis, for example, has claimed that the bulk of historical personages who figure in the *chansons de geste* lived during the eighth, ninth, and tenth centuries, and he argues that the memory of these figures would have been preserved or added only in oral, popular songs— no *jongleur* steeped in the oral tradition, he holds, would have worked from a written text.[13] Other evidence has appeared in fragments of documents, such as the so-called *Nota Emilianense*, which recounts in a few Latin sentences the story of Ronceval and mentions Roland's death.[14] The manuscript dates from the third quarter of the eleventh century, but its content was probably composed at an earlier time. This fragment attests to the existence of legends about Roland (whatever their form) that predate the Oxford version of the tale.

The culmination of traditionalism was reached in 1959 with the publication in French of a gigantic work by a Spanish scholar named Ramón Menéndez Pidal, entitled *La Chanson de Roland et la tradition épique des Francs*. A real heavyweight, this book contains information about all the history and documents that so far have been concerned with the question of *Roland*'s origins. Pidal's goal is to establish how the original tale of Roland might have expanded as each successive age made its characteristic contribution to the narrative. Although many readers will find Pidal's book "unliterary" in its response to poetry and somewhat obsessively conceived, the book is one of the most valuable for its wealth of historical information.

Bédier and Pidal are the great extremists, then, in the polemic over the origins of the *Song of Roland*. Both critics concede, at times, that there is perhaps a middle ground to the question.[15] This middle ground is subtle and rich with complexities and has become the terrain of a number of critics who see no real contradiction between poetry that draws heavily on convention for its content and poetry where the genius of an individual has intervened. Consequently, the last few years have brought a number of books whose positions are eclectic and conciliatory, constituting what we might now call "soft-line traditionalism." [16] Scholars are more discriminating about their working vocabulary nowadays, and words such as *jongleur, cantilène, rédacteur* ("revisor"), "chronicle," and "legend" are no longer accepted as sacrosanct categories.[17] Current scholars shy away from iron-bound conclusions and prefer to grapple with individual textual problems, where subtle and shaded opinions are valued. Scholars also tend to be less emotional about the question of how *original* a version may be: a poet is no less an artist for arranging his inherited material instead of creating it all by himself.

In my opinion, the gradual movement away from the time-worn polemic about origins is welcome.[18] Who cannot but feel dismay at the fact that perhaps three quarters of the scholarship about the *Song of Roland* is really about the poem's *pre*history and yet has finally been able to prove nothing that is conclusive about its author or the exact circumstances of its composition? Indeed, one occasionally discerns moments of frustration and impatience even among the great polemicists themselves. Joseph Bédier, the most brilliant of all, voices a kind of disillusionment about the value of his scholarly achievement at the end of the fourth volume of his *Legendes épiques.* As tired as Charlemagne himself, Bédier pines (sincerely, I believe) for the intellectual freedom that he has for so many years denied himself:

> My success has been only very imperfect, I know. How many questions I asked without solving them! How many questions I perceived, without even daring to ask them! What connection is there between the *chansons de geste* and the nearly contemporaneous romances of the cycle of antiquity and the cycle of Brittany? Why, in the *chansons de geste,* does the Christian supernatural give way so suddenly to the marvels of fairy land; why does the epic evolve so quickly into romance? Others will seek and find the answers. Others will discover between the *chansons de geste* and other contemporary forms of poetry and of art, relationships which are finer, more numerous, and more subtle.[19]

Indeed, one often has the impression while reading Bédier that his intellectual powers were somewhat mismatched with the task that he set for himself. May we not take his lament, therefore, as license for shifting our concerns away from the question of origins and for raising new questions about the *Song of Roland?*

⋐⋟ APPENDIX IV ⋘⋟

FURTHER READING

For the reader who wishes to acquaint himself with the *Song of Roland* in more detail, I offer a short list of useful material to consult. The most accessible edition of the poem is Bédier's, which first appeared in 1922. Not only does it respect the textual order of the Oxford manuscript but includes a face-to-face translation into modern French. Some readers may prefer R. Mortier's edition in the series that he edited, *Les textes de la Chanson de Roland*, 10 vols., Paris, 1940–41. A phototype reproduction of the manuscript has been edited by Laborde, accompanied by a paleographical study by Charles Samaran, Paris, 1932. A recent bibliographical survey of criticism about the *chanson de geste* in general and the *Song of Roland* in particular will be found in the section by Knudsen and Misrahi in the useful guide, *The Medieval Literature of Western Europe, A Review of Recent Research, Mainly 1930–1960*, ed. John H. Fisher, New York, 1966. Though extremely selective, this chapter has the merit of situating specific references in a context of broader critical concern.

For the student who does not know French, relatively few secondary sources in English will raise the kind of fundamental questions that I consider necessary for a healthy critical initiation into the poem. The most notable exception is of course Erich Auerbach's *Mimesis: The Representation of Reality in Western Literature*, New York, 1953. One chapter in this book contains a brilliant stylistic study of the *Roland*. Another stylistic study, more recent, by Stephen G. Nichols, Jr., has a self-explanatory title: *Formulaic Diction and Thematic Composition in the Chanson de Roland*, a monograph published at Chapel Hill, N.C., 1961. Students interested in techniques of oral composition will especially profit from A. B. Lord's invaluable book, *The Singer of Tales*, Cambridge, 1960, which is a continuation of the work initiated by Milman Parry. An informal book by Jesse Crosland, *The Old French Epic*, New York, 1951, will serve as an introduction to the genre. A book by George Fenwick Jones, *The Ethos of the Song of Roland*, Baltimore, Md., 1965, will provide the reader with occasional (though not always convincing) insights, especially in the form of semantic details. An excellent and recent book about *chansons de geste* composed after the *Song of Roland* offers much good hindsight on the poem: William C. Calin, *The Old French Epic of Revolt*, Geneva, 1962. Finally, readers will find in the notes references to various articles in English which I found useful in this book.

The reader versed in French will find Pierre Le Gentil's book, *La chanson de Roland*, Paris, 1955 (reprinted in 1967), the best introduction to all aspects of the poem, and it includes a bibliography. It has been recently translated by Francis F. Beer, under the title, *The Chanson de Roland*, Cambridge, 1969. Most readers will find it difficult to avoid for long the question about the poem's origins. A summary of the problem will be found in Italo Siciliano's *Les origines des chansons de geste*, trans. Antonetti, Paris, 1951. However, readers will find consolation in learning that some very sensitive readings of the poem have grown out of this polemic. The last two volumes of Joseph Bédier's *Les légendes épiques*, 4 vols., Paris, 1908–13, are frequently brilliant; see also his useful handbook, *La chanson de Roland commentée*, Paris, 1927, which includes a glossary by Lucien Foulet. Two other older books are still very worthwhile: Robert Fawtier's *La chanson de Roland*, Paris, 1933; and Edmond Faral's *La chanson de Roland, étude et analyse*, Paris, 1933. Three more recent books have made real contributions to our understanding of the poem. Martín de Riquer's *Les chansons de geste françaises*, translated from the Spanish by I. Cluzel, Paris, 1957, contains a summary of the debate over the poem's origins as well as a good introduction to the poem and its historical background. Ramón Menéndez Pidal's *La chanson de Roland et la tradition épique des Francs*, trans. I. Cluzel, 1960, is perhaps the definitive statement of traditionalism. It includes massive information and a substantial bibliography. Jules Horrent's *La chanson de Roland dans les littératures française et espagnole au moyen age*, Brussels, 1951, is valuable as an exemplary study of textual problems and as a source of bibliography. The best stylistic study of the poem is Jean Rychner's *La chanson de geste, essai sur l'art épique des jongleurs*, Geneva, 1955. Other stylistic studies will be found in *La technique littéraire des chansons de geste, actes du colloque de Liège, Septembre, 1957*, Paris, 1959. A more recent but less innovative study of the formulaic narrative of warfare in the *chansons de geste* is Renate Hitze's *Studien zu Sprache und Stil der Kampfschilderungen in den Chansons de Geste*, Geneva, 1965. On the iconography of the *Song of Roland* in medieval art, see the luxuriously illustrated publication of Rita Lejeune and Jacques Stiennon, *La légende de Roland dans l'art du moyen âge*, 2 vols., Brussels, 1966.

Two recent books in German deserve praise. Matthias Waltz's *Rolandslied, Wilhelmslied, Alexiuslied*, Heidelberg, 1965, has a section on the *Roland*, which is both penetrating and circumspect. Karl-Heinz Bender's book, *König und Vassal*, Heidelberg, 1967, considers the *Song of Roland* in the light of eleventh-century political and religious ideology.

In many ways the student will find a reading of Homer's *Iliad* the most seminal approach to the *Song of Roland* because of the cultural analogies it suggests; it goes without saying that the best Homeric scholarship will be indirectly beneficial to readers of Old French epic.

⊸§ NOTES ⹀

Chapter II

1. See the brilliant chapter by Erich Auerbach, *"Excursus: Gloria Passionis,"* in *Literary Language and Its Public,* English trans. Willard Trask, New York, 1965, pp. 67–81.

2. Ramón Menéndez Pidal, *La Chanson de Roland et la tradition épique des Francs,* trans. I. Cluzel, Paris, 1960, pp. 348–50, gives a more detailed summary and bibliography of the question.

3. Pidal, *Roland et la tradition épique,* p. 398.

4. Joseph Bédier, *La Chanson de Roland commentée,* Paris, 1927, p. 6 (hereafter cited as *Commentaires*).

5. Pidal, *Roland et la tradition épique,* p. 401.

6. All translations are my own and are based on Joseph Bédier's edition, Paris, 1922.

7. Edmond Faral, *La Chanson de Roland, étude et analyse,* Paris, 1933, p. 247.

8. Pidal, *Roland et la tradition épique,* pp. 346–47.

9. Pidal, *Roland et la tradition épique,* p. 93.

10. We have no way of knowing whether the poets of the oral tradition subscribed to any formal critical postulates. I suspect that they did not. However, the question of narrative order (*dispositio*) is much discussed in medieval poetic theory. After the Carolingian period, "natural order" (*dispositio naturalis*) meant the order of events as they really occurred in time, and was opposed to "artificial order" (*dispositio artificialis*), which meant the reordering of events in poetic fiction. Virgil's *Aeneid* was a model of artificial order for medieval poets. His example was consciously followed by medieval poets in the Latin tradition, and perhaps unconsciously by poets in the vernacular tradition as well. See E. de Bruyne, *Etudes d'esthétique médiévale,* 3 vols., Brugges, 1946, Vol. I, p. 231; also, E. Faral, *Les arts poétiques du XIIᵉ et du XIIIᵉ siècle,* Paris, 1962, pp. 54–60.

11. Bédier, *Commentaires,* p. 96.

12. The whole question of how the poet of *Roland* understood the notion of time is fascinating and has provoked diverging responses among critics. The discussion centers for the most part around the poet's use of tenses in his narrative. Naturally, critics are challenged by the apparent random use of tenses to discover some underlying concept of time to account for the confusion that the modern reader is certain to feel. In my opinion, no critic has divulged a consistent or convincing system. More attention to this problem is in order, especially from modern

109

linguists who have new tools for analysis. There is not space here to enter into the details of theories that have evolved in the past, but the reader will find a convenient and provocative summary of research on this question in a recent book, which is valuable also for its bibliography: Friederike Stefenelli-Fürst, *Die Tempora der Vergangenheit in der Chanson de Geste*, Vienna, 1966.

Chapter III

1. For a convenient linguistic survey of the poem, see Bédier's *Commentaires*, pp. 241–62.

2. Milman Parry, "Studies in the Epic Technique of Oral Verse-Making, I: Homer and Homeric Style," in *Harvard Studies in Classical Philology*, Vol. 41, 1930, p. 80. This definition has been accepted without reserve by certain students of oral epic for two generations. As we shall see in the discussion that follows, formulas do *not* always appear under the same metrical conditions, but can be dilated to any length, depending upon the will of the poet. Parry's definition of an oral "formula" is very narrow.

3. Marc Bloch's *Feudal Society*, 2 vols., Chicago, 1956–57, is still the most authoritative history of this period.

4. See the meticulous study of formulaic battle narrative in the *chanson de geste* by Renate Hitze, *Studien zu Sprache und Stil der Kampfschilderungen in den Chansons de Geste*, Geneva and Paris, 1965.

5. Adam Parry, "The Language of Achilles," in *Transactions and Proceedings of the American Philological Association*, Vol. 87, 1956, p. 3.

6. Richmond Lattimore, trans., *Iliad*, Chicago, 1951, Book IX, ll. pp. 312–14.

7. Parry, "Language of Achilles."

8. George Fenwick Jones, *The Ethos of the Song of Roland*, Baltimore, Md., 1963, pp. 20–21.

9. See Paul Zumther's historico-linguistic study, *Langue et techniques poétiques à l'époque romane*, Paris, 1963, esp. pp. 38–55.

10. I refer to Erich Auerbach's well-known thesis in *Mimesis*, Chap. 5.

11. Eupolemius, *The Messiad*, ed. Manitius, *Romanische Förschungen* 6, 1891, pp. 509–56.

12. Latin, the language of Bible and the liturgy, was capable of its own kind of action—spiritual action as opposed to physical. *Grammatica* is the medium of salvation. In the words of one monastic grammarian who comments on the *Rule* of St. Benedict,

> This little book is full of holy gifts; it contains Scripture and it is seasoned with grammar. Scripture teaches us to seek after the kingdom of God, to detach the self from the earth, to rise above the self. It promises the blessed these heavenly boons: to live with the Lord, to dwell always with Him. Grammar, then, through the goodness of God, confers great benefits on those who read it with care (Smaragdus of St. Mihiel, as quoted by Jean Leclerq, *The Love of Learning and the Desire for God*, New York, 1961, p. 52).

Chapter IV

1. I recommend Jean Rychner's book, *La chanson de geste: essai sur l'art épique des jongleurs*, Geneva, 1955, as the best stylistic study of the *Song of Roland*. I rely on this book for many of the ideas in this chapter, including the diagram.

2. A shorter, but equally penetrating stylistic study of the *Song of Roland*, concerned particularly with the problem of narrative continuity, is to be found in Eugène Vinaver's article, "La mort de Roland," in *Cahiers de civilisation médiévale* (hereafter abbreviated *CCM*), Vol. 6, 1964, pp. 133–34.

3. This again is a theme, contested nowadays by some, of Chapter 5 in Erich Auerbach's great stylistic study, *Mimesis*.

Chapter V

1. In general, the discipline of logic is lacking, not only in vernacular literature of the eleventh century, but in monastic literature as well. Scholasticism, which had not yet imposed itself, was largely responsible for the rise of logical thought in the later middle ages. Leclerq (*Love of Learning*, p. 80) says, "This is true of many monastic authors; they do not always compose after a logical pattern which has been definitely fixed upon in advance. Within the literary form chosen, they make use of the utmost freedom. The plan really follows from a psychological development, determined by the plan of associations."

2. This quarrel, as well as the earlier one, has been variously interpreted. For a discussion of its possible implications, see A. Burger, "Les deux scènes du cor dans la *Chanson de Roland*," in *La technique littéraire des chansons de geste,* Paris, 1959, pp. 105–26.

3. Cf. Saint Paul, I Cor. 13:4.

4. Saint Paul, Col. 3:14.

5. D. W. Robertson, Jr., *A Preface to Chaucer*, Princeton, N.J., 1960, pp. 164–65.

6. I have treated this idea at greater length in the following article: "Spatial Structure in the *Chanson de Roland*," in *Modern Language Notes*, Vol. 82, 1967, pp. 604–23.

7. *The Holy Bible, Revised Standard Edition*, New York, 1952, Psalm 121.

8. See the article by Allain Renoir, "Roland's Lament," *Speculum*, Vol. 35, 1960, pp. 572–83.

9. Auerbach, *Mimesis*, p. 96.

10. Jules Horrent, *La Chanson de Roland dans les littératures française et espagnole au moyen-âge*, Brussels, 1954, p. 267.

11. See the article by Charles Muscatine, "The Locus of Action in Medieval Narrative," *Romance Philology*, Vol. 17, 1963, pp. 155–22. See also, "The Emergence of Psychological Allegory in Old French Romance," *PMLA*, Vol. 68, 1953, pp. 1160–82.

12. For a study of the heroic ideal in the Anglo-Saxon poem, see the article by George Clark, "The Battle of Maldon: A Heroic Poem," *Speculum*, Vol. 43, 1968, pp. 52–71.

13. Joseph Bédier, *Légendes épiques*, Paris, 1908–13, Vol. IV, p. 444.

Chapter VI

1. Brackets mine, and the insertion follows Bédier's interpolation of a lacuna in the text.

2. Lattimore, trans., *Iliad*, Bk. VIII, l. 306; also Virgil's *Aeneid*, trans. L. R. Lind, Bloomington, 2nd ed., 1962, Bk. IX, l. 433.

3. See the article by P. Zumthor, "Etude typologique des planctus contenus dans

la *Chanson de Roland,"* in *La technique littéraire des chansons de geste,* Paris, 1959, pp. 219–35.   ,

Chapter VII

1. For a survey of epics in the cycle of Charlemagne, see Martin de Riquer, *Les chansons de geste françaises,* French trans. I. Cluzel, Paris, 1957.

2. One should be careful not to imagine that such a role for the individual artist is restricted to oral poets of the *chanson de geste:* most early medieval art is anonymous; analogous attitudes exist, moreover, even in the literary tradition of biblical commentators:

> The memory, fashioned wholly by the Bible and nurtured entirely by biblical words and the images they evoke, causes them to express themselves entirely in a biblical vocabulary. Reminiscences are not quotations, elements of phrases borrowed from another. They are the words of the person using them; they belong to him. (Leclerq, *Love of Learning,* p. 81).

3. For arguments against the authenticity of the Baligant episode, see Pidal, *Roland et la tradition épique,* pp. 121–24; also Horrent, *Roland dans littératures française et espagnole,* pp. 120–34.

4. See, for example, Paul Aebischer's article, "Pour la défense et l'illustration de l'épisode de Baligant," reprinted in his collection entitled, *Rolandiana et Oliveriana,* Geneva, 1967, pp. 211–20.

5. History's verdict on Charlemagne's rule was not by any means unanimous; indeed, *chansons de geste* such as *La chanson de Guillaume* depict Charlemagne as a figure of weakness who is unable to sustain justice in his kingdom. For a good, general discussion of the theme of empire and Carolingianism, see Robert Folz, *L'idée de l'Empire en occident,* Paris, 1953.

6. The reader will find the following book useful as a source of post-Carolingian ideology: Robert Folz, *Le souvenir et la légende de Charlemagne dans l'Empire germanique médiéval,* Paris, 1950. Karl-Heinz Bender, in his book *König und Vassal,* Heidelberg, 1967, studies the theme of Carolingianism specifically in the *Song of Roland;* see pp. 9–42.

7. My translation is from Bédier's *Légendes épiques,* Vol. IV, p. 456.

8. St. Augustine, *The City of God,* trans. Marcus Dods, New York, 1950, Book XI, ch. 17, p. 159.

9. St. Augustine, *City of God,* ch. 18, p. 160.

Chapter VIII

1. For a good discussion of the significance of Ganelon's trial, see John Halverson's article, "The Trial of Ganelon," *Speculum,* Vol. 42, 1967, pp. 661–69. Halverson sees the conflict of issues as one involving Germanic tribalism and Capetian nationalism. I doubt whether the poet himself perceived the problem with such ideological clarity. See also William Calin's *The Old French Epic of Revolt,* Geneva, 1962, for another discussion of these political problems as seen in the *chansons de geste.*

2. See Bender, *König und Vassal,* pp. 33–36.

3. See the exemplary little article by Adalbert Dessau, "L'idée de la trahison

au moyen âge," in *CCM*, Vol. III, 1960, 24. I am happy to acknowledge his contributions to portions of the present chapter.

4. Halverson, "Trial of Ganelon," p. 661.

5. See Dessau, "L'idée de la trahison," p. 25, whose comments I paraphrase in this paragraph.

6. This point rests on evidence shown to me by Gerald Bond, in an unpublished graduate paper on the trial of Ganelon.

7. Scholars have attempted to discover in the judicial procedure against Ganelon some clue to when the *Roland* may have been composed. Their success has been thwarted, however, by the possibility that archaisms in the poem could very well have been deliberate. The most extensive study of the trial is by Ruggero Ruggieri, *Il processo di Gano*, Florence, 1936.

8. Ruggieri, *Il processo di Gano*, p. 103.

9. Geoffrey Chaucer, "The Book of the Duchess," ed. F. N. Robinson, Cambridge, 1957, p. 277, ll. 1121–23.

10. For interesting observations about the notion of character in the *chanson de geste*, see Calin's *Old French Epic of Revolt*.

Appendix II

1. The text in question may conveniently be consulted in the appendix in Pidal, *Roland et la tradition épique*, p. 526.

2. Einhard, *The Life of Charlemagne*, trans. Sydney Painter, Ann Arbor, Mich., 1966, p. 334.

3. For a summary of the data relating to the historical personage of Roland, see Pidal, *Roland et la tradition épique*, pp. 215, 406–11.

Appendix III

1. I stress that I can hardly begin to summarize the arguments that have accumulated through generations of critics. More complete summaries exist, most notable of which is Italo Siciliano's witty account of existing theories about the poem's origins. I refer the reader to the French translation from the Italian by P. Antonetti: *Les origines des chansons de geste*, Paris, 1951. More recent summaries will be found in the French translation of a book by Martín de Riquer, *Les Chansons de geste françaises*, trans. I. Cluzel, Paris, 1957, pp. 34–52; and in Pidal, *Roland et la tradition épique*, pp. 3–50.

2. For a lengthier account of the poem's discovery, see Pierre Le Gentil, *La chanson de Roland*, Paris, 1967, pp. 6–8.

3. For a concise statement of Paris' theory, see his review of Pio Rajna, *Le origini dell' epopea francese*, Florence, 1884, in *Romania*, Vol. 13, 1887, pp. 616–19.

4. See note above for reference.

5. For a history of this inversion in critical theory during the romantic period, see M. H. Abrams, *The Mirror and the Lamp*, Oxford, 1953.

6. Bédier, *Légendes épiques*, Vols. III and IV.

7. See Bédier's citation of Karl Voretsch in Vol. IV, p. 342, for an example of the attitude against which Bédier was reacting.

8. Bédier, *Légendes épiques*, Vol. III, p. 290.

9. Bédier, *Commentaires*, p. 30.

10. Faral, *La chanson de Roland*.

11. Albert Pauphilet, "Sur la *Chanson de Roland*," *Romania*, Vol. 59, 1933, p. 171.

12. See Maurice Willmotte, *Epopée française, origine et élaboration*, Paris, 1939.

13. René Louis, "L'epopée française est carolingienne," in *Colloquios de Roncesvalles, Agosto*, 1955, Saragossa, 1956, p. 452.

14. Published by D. Alonso, "La primitiva epica francesa a la luz de una Nota Emilianense," *Revista de Filologia Espanola*, Vol. XXXVII, 1953, pp. 1–94.

15. See Bedier, *Légendes épiques*, Vol. III, p. 446; also, Pidal, *Roland et la tradition épique*, p. 73.

16. See, for example, Horrent, *Roland dans les littératures française et espagnole;* Maurice Delbouille, *Sur la genèse de la chanson de Roland*, Brussels, 1954; Pierre Le Gentil, *La chanson de Roland*, Paris, 1955 (reissued in 1967), p. 90.

17. See Jean Frappier, "Réflexions sur les rapports des chansons de geste et de l'histoire," in *Zeitschrift für romanische Philologie*, Vol. 73, 1957, p. 12.

18. A recent and interesting exception to this is Barton Sholod's book, *Charlemagne in Spain: the Cultural Legacy of Roncesvalles*, Geneva and Paris, 1966. Sholod believes that the heavily Frankified territory between Septimania and Spain, as well as a ninth-century Frankish interest in the evolving cult of Santiago, caused the legend of Roland to thrive in these areas in the form of oral epic. "The truly inventive impulse behind the *Roland* is a tenth-century phenomenon, in which historical characters and incidents, designed to lend a spirit of contemporaneousness to the changing poems, were continually added in the process" (p. 227).

19. Bédier, *Légendes épiques*, Vol. IV, p. 476.

INDEX

A

Abrams, M. H., 113
Aebischer, Paul, 112
Aix (Aachen), 4–5, 7, 11, 74, 82
Al Arabi, 96–97
Alonso, D., 114
Al Rahman, 96
Apostles, The, 9
Ariosto, Ludovico, 1
Arthur, King, 1, 9, 98
Aude, 46, 52, 58
Auerbach, Erich, 106, 109–111
Aventure, 11

B

Babylon, 72
Baligant, 7, 37, 75, 77, 79, 103
Baligant episode, 67, 72–76, 77, 79, 103
Basile and Basant, 5, 11
Basques, 97
Battle of Malden, The, 63
    Byrhtnoth, 63
Bédier, Joseph, 63, 102–9, 111–114
Beer, Francis F., 107
Bender, Karl-Heinz, 108, 112
Beowulf, 23, 89, 92
Bible, The: 72
    Book of Daniel, 60, 74
    Judas, 83
    Lazarus, 60
    Satan, 83
Blancandrin, 4–5, 19, 36
Bloch, Marc, 110

Boiardo, M. M., 1
Bramimonde, 7, 80–81, 90
Burger, A., 111

C

Calidore, 89
Calin, William C., 107, 112–113
Cantilène, 101, 105
Capetians, 81
Carolingian Empire, 26, 74, 76
Cervantes, Miguel de, *Don Quixote*, 92
Charity, 52–53, 87, 91
Charlemagne, 2, 4, 5–19, 26, 29–33, 35,
    37, 39–41, 44–46, 51–54, 56, 63–77,
    82–87, 89, 90–93, 96–98, 102
Chateaubriand, 101
Chaucer, Geoffrey, 88, 101, 113
Chrétien de Troyes, 52
    Perceval, 11
    Yvain, 62
Christ, 2, 9, 35, 56, 74–75, 79, 91
    Anti-Christ, 74
Christians, 8–9, 11–12, 15, 23, 25, 31, 35,
    43, 48, 60, 73, 76, 79, 83–84, 86–87,
    90–91, 93
Clark, George, 111
Cluzel, I., 107
Comedy, 64
Crosland, Jesse, 106

D

Dante, 88
    The Divine Comedy, 8

de Bruyne, E., 109
Delbouille, Maurice, 114
Démesure, 60
Demonic parody, 79
Dessau, Adalbert, 112–113
Discourse, 13, 31–38, 51, 59, 62
Dispositio, 109
Dostoevesky's *Crime and Punishment*:
  Alyosha Karamazov, 11

E

Ebro River, 6, 65, 97
Einhard (Eginhard), 97
Eupolemius, 110
  The Messiad, 37

F

Fainting, 57, 69
Faral, Edmond, 107, 109, 114
Fawtier, Robert, 107
Fehderecht, 84
Feudalism, 9, 22, 25, 33, 35–36, 60, 62–63,
  67, 69, 74, 81–88, 93
Fisher, John H., 106
Folz, Robert, 112
Formulaic diction, 21, 24–30, 34–36, 39,
  66, 76, 93, 104
Fortitudo et sapientia, 14, 51, 60
Foulet, Lucien, 107
Franco-Prussian War, 102
Frappier, Jean, 114
Frederick I, 74

G

Ganelon, 3–5, 7, 9–10, 13–19, 28, 32–33,
  36, 39, 41–42, 45, 50, 64, 67, 77, 81–
  89
Grammatica, 110

H

Halverson, John, 112–13
Hero, heroism, 12–14, 19–20, 22, 25–34,
  36–38, 40, 44, 47, 49–52, 56, 58–71,
  73–76, 85, 88–89, 92–93

Hitze, Renate, 107, 110
Holy Grail, The, 62
Homer, 1, 8, 25, 48, 56, 103
  The Iliad, 1–2, 8, 21, 31–33, 36, 68,
    89–90, 98, 108
    Achilles, 8–9, 14, 32–33, 38, 56, 70,
     90
    Hector, 56
    Nestor, 89
    Patroclus, 14, 56, 70
    Priam, 89, 91
  The Odyssey, 31–32, 87, 108
Honor, 6, 14, 19, 50, 60, 83, 85, 87, 92
Horace, 36
Horrent, Jules, 107, 111–112, 114
Hruodlandus, 98
Hugo, Victor, 101

I

"individualism," 103–105
In medias res, 4, 47

J

Jones, George Fenwick, 106, 110
Jongleur, 8, 104–105
Judicial duel, 85–87

L

Lattimore, Richmond, 110–111
Lawrence, D. H., *Sons and Lovers*:
  Paul Morel, 11
Leclerq, Jean, 110–112
Le Gentil, Pierre, 107, 113–114
Le Jeune, Rita, 108
Lind, L. R., 111
Lord, A. B., 106
Louis, René, 104, 114
Lucan, 103

M

Marsile, 4, 7, 11, 16–17, 19, 32, 49, 72,
  77, 80, 90
Michel, Francisque, 101

Milton, John, 27
  Paradise Lost, 36
  Paradise Regained, 1
Mortier, R., 106
"Munjoie!", 79
Muscatine, Charles, 111

N

Naimes, Duke of, 4, 14–15
Nichols, Stephen G., Jr., 106
Nota Emilianense, 104

O

Oliphant, 6
Oliver, 5–6, 9–10, 14–16, 23–25, 27–28, 33, 42–44, 46–48, 50–53, 56–59, 63, 65, 69, 78–79, 83, 85
  Olivarius, Oliverius, 9
Oral poetry, 9, 21–24, 37, 54, 73, 81, 104
Origins, theory of, 8–9, 21, 72, 81–82, 100–105
"Oxford Version," 8, 15–19, 21, 42, 61, 72, 80, 98, 101

P

Paris, Gaston, 101, 113
Parry, Adam, 33, 110
Parry, Milman, 106, 110
Pauphilet, Albert, 114
Pidal, Ramón Menéndez, 104, 107, 109, 112–113
Pinabel, 7, 84–88, 91
Planctus, 68–69
"*Précieuse!*", 79

Q

Question rolandienne, la, 99, 104

R

Rajna, Pio, 102, 113
Revenge, 16, 18, 66, 82–84, 89, 91

Riquer, Martín de, 107, 113
Robertson, D. W., Jr., 111
Rodlan, 98
Roland, 4–5, 7–19, 24–33, 35, 38–39, 43–44, 46–74, 79, 83–87, 89, 92, 98, 102, 104
Romance, 52, 62, 80, 93
Romance of the Rose, 62
Romanesque, 11, 25, 41
Romantic movement, 100–102
Rome, 74, 96
Ronceval, 5–6, 8–9
Rothlandus, 97
Round Table, The, 1, 9
Royal Annals Until 829, 97
Ruggieri, Ruggero, 113
Rule of St. Benedict, The, 62
Rychner, Jean, 107, 110

S

St. Augustine, 112
  The City of God, 79–80
  The Confessions, 8
St. Bernard, 62
St. Gabriel, 60, 62, 64
St. Michael, 60, 62, 64
St. Paul, 52, 111
Samaran, Charles, 106
Sapienta, 14
Saxons, 96–97
Shakespeare's *Hamlet*, 11
Sholod, Barton, 114
Siciliano, Italo, 107, 113
Sidney, Sir Philip, 1
Spenser, Edmund, 77
  The Faerie Queene, 78
  Calidore, 89
Stael, Madame de, 101
Stefenelli-Furst, 110
Stiennon, Jacques, 108

T

Tasso, Torquato, 77
  Gerusalemme Liberata, 78
Teutonism, 102

Thierry, 7, 85–87, 91
Time, the notion of, 11, 13, 17, 71, 109–110
"traditionalism," 101, 103–105
Tragedy, 10, 18, 29–30, 40, 53–56, 63–71, 75, 81, 87, 89–93
Treason, 82–84, 86–88
Tristan and Isolde, 86
Troy, 1, 98
Turold, 9
Turpin, 1, 5–6, 15, 25, 47, 51, 102

U

Unity (The Unities), 2, 40, 67–68, 72–73, 82
Urban II, 74

V

Vinaver, Eugène, 111
Virgil, 47, 103
  The Aeneid, 8, 78, 103, 109
  Aeneas, 41, 76
  Romulus, 89
  Turnus, 76
Voretsch, Karl, 113

W

Waltz, Matthias, 108
Wilmotte, Maurice, 114

Z

Zumthor, Paul, 110–111